To my mom whose unconditional love kept us sane.

To my brother who stood in front of me and took it.

To my husband who never stopped loving me.

Linda, Everyone has a story and it sounds like ours is similar. You were a delight to meet and I can tell you are a delight to be. Always, Audrey ♡

ACKNOWLEDGMENTS:

Thank you

To Baxter Kruger who read my first draft
and encouraged me to dig deeper.

To Debbie Sawczak
who edited my first draft.

To Sharon Tang
for the caricature drawing on the cover.

LIFE WITH LES

(INTRODUCTION)

The large shadow that glided ominously above the modest group of neatly clad mourners disappeared almost as quickly as it had appeared. The pilot never noticed the family and friends huddled among the rows of etched stones standing at attention to honor heroes of long ago. He never heard the lyrics of the all-too-familiar hymn sung by the grieving, their voices muted by the sputter of his single-engine plane. And if he did notice, what was that to him? Hadn't he made these routine maneuvers a couple of dozen times, and hadn't there always been folks below dressed in Sunday best standing arm in arm on freshly dug dirt? He was too high to see the tissues in their hands, but what he could see was a seemingly infinite number of tiny white rectangles in evenly spaced rows, nestled among the rolling hills of the Cemetery for Soldiers of Foreign Wars. But this meant nothing to him. It was close to noon, and he was hungry.

The one-by-two-foot monuments were endless. Column after column of neat, simple, headstones, locatable only by number, were not representative of the dead that lay beneath: each life memorialized by a small white marker was unique and complex. Certainly the life of my father (the man we had come to bury) was by no means nowhere near as orderly as the manicured grounds and cookie-cutter headstones of the cemetery.

The picture-perfect surroundings that lay above him did not match his life. They only matched the peace we hoped he had finally found in his new home not made by human hands. Perhaps the life we were remembering was not one lived well on many counts, but it was a life that had been worth living. It was a life that had given us many stories— some beautiful, some not so beautiful. We had gathered to share those stories, and the sound of the small plane fading into the distance served to remind us of the man whose memory would never fade, and whose life would never cease to be a part of our own.

THE GRAVESIDE

The young man stood beside the marker, half smiling and with a slight quiver in his voice as he summoned us forward for the graveside service. He began by thanking everyone, all fifteen of us, gathered on the hay-strewn mud that kept us from getting close to the newly dug grave.

"Thank you for coming to honor my grandfather today. Of course, most of you are family, but we appreciate the good friends that came as well. I've been asked to say a few words about our grandfather, dad, and friend."

His six-foot-two frame, boyish good looks, and undeniable charm reminded me of some of the pictures I had boxed up of my dad, taken when he was a Lieutenant in the Air Corps during World War II. Though not as tall as my son, my dad was quite handsome and had winning ways, especially when it came to the opposite sex.

My dad loved the ladies, especially the ones on the silver screen. I remember watching old movies with him late at night and wanting to be as beautiful as Lana Turner, Ava Gardner, and Grace Kelly, because those were the women my dad always talked about. I remember him pointing out their lovely features, and wondered if he would ever look at me the way he looked at them. There was one lady, however, that beat them all, and that was my mom. I had heard my dad say over and over how beautiful he thought she was, and how it had been love at first sight when he had met her while stationed in Bakers Field, California.

My mom lived in San Francisco at the time, with her parents and two older brothers. One afternoon while my dad was on furlough, riding through the streets of Mission District, he spotted a brown-eyed beauty with dark, shoulder-length hair like Ava Gardner's and an hourglass figure like Lana Turner's. Little did he know at the time how lucky he would be to get not only the most sought-after girl in the neighborhood, but one who would stay beside him with grace and patience through thick and much thin. In this way she would outlast and outshine all the Grace Kellys on the planet.

Just a month shy of seventy-two years, their marriage was a remarkable journey for us all—for them as a couple, and also for the two kids they brought into this world, who gave them five grandchildren and six great-grandchildren. They lived a very ordinary life in many respects, but the way it shaped and impacted my own made it unique to me. This is a story about growing up with a man who made me laugh one minute and cry the next. It is a story of love, forgiveness, instruction, and pain, about a family that many would call dysfunctional, yet one I would not trade for all the families in the world.

I can say that now. Growing up I did not always feel that way, and neither did my brother. And as I have sat down recently to listen to my mom recall her life with this very unique man, I can tell you there were days she wished for something else as well.

"Today we have come together to bury our grandfather," my son continued, nodding to his cousin, Jack.

He knew Jack was taking the death of my dad harder than anyone, except for maybe my mom. Jack was very close to his grandfather. He was the preacher in the family, and it was no surprise that my dad had requested that Jack conduct the funeral service. It was my mom's wish that her other grandson, Elliot, conduct the graveside service. She had wanted my oldest son, Michael, to say a few words as well, but unforeseen circumstances had taken him and his family back to their home in Charlotte earlier than expected. Michael had said his goodbyes the day before, and now it was Elliot's turn. He cleared his throat.

"Gathered here today are our family and a few friends, who came to celebrate with us the life of Les Wilson."

My dad was 95 years old when he took his last breath. At that age, there are not many friends, or even family members, who are still alive and can attend a funeral. Most of his cousins and friends had already checked out a long time ago. He had one cousin or two still left behind in nursing homes. Nursing homes! You can't live without them, but you have a hard time living with them. My mom had prayed we would never have to put dad in a nursing home, and her prayers had been answered: he died one week after entering the Castle Heights Rehabilitation Unit in Lebanon. Interestingly enough, this was the exact location in which he had trained as a liaison pilot during the war. It was fitting that he should die on the very spot that had given him the greatest sense of purpose.

He had loved serving in the Air Corps. For a man with a soaring spirit and an Errol Flynn outlook on life, it was the perfect scenario. It was the only time in his otherwise undisciplined life that he submitted to some form of order, but only because he had no choice: either you did what the Air Corps said, or you were thrown out by the seat of your neatly pleated pants. The Air Corps gave him something he'd never had before: a uniform and respect. It also gave him plenty of stories to tell us over and over again.

One such story was the encounter he had with Jimmy Stewart. To hear my dad tell it, they were best friends. The famous actor had enlisted in the service and was a big hit among all the men. Dad loved to tell how Mr. Stewart would sit at the same mess table and converse with him about different movies and fellow actors. "Jimmy Stewart was one of the nicest guys you could ever meet," Dad said. Every year as we watched "It's a Wonderful Life," Dad would recount how Jimmy Stewart had shared his soap with him one evening after all-day maneuvers. During Dad's last months, he took the time to write a personal letter to Mr. Stewart, recalling some of the events from their stint in the service together. He never heard back.

The service took Dad away from his mom, to whom he was very attached. Grandma had raised Dad practically all by herself. Life wasn't always easy for her as a single mom who had picked cotton as a young girl and worked her way up to a cosmetic assembly line worker in her brother's petroleum jelly factory. My dad, on the other hand, had it made, as my grandmother pretty much spoiled him; not with money, because they never had much of that, but by letting him get his own way.

My dad's father, a very good-looking man, had been quite a rounder, cheating on my grandmother and getting the other woman pregnant while still married to my grandmother. He was a womanizer, a drinker, and an irresponsible provider who left my grandmother with a small child and an infant. Dad's sister died while still a baby; she got sick, and Grandma couldn't care properly for her or pay for sufficient medical care. The baby's death left my dad as her only child as well as the only man in her life, a circumstance that made for a very interesting upbringing with implications for all our lives. I'm not sure what made life more complicated for us: the fact that my brother and I were raised by three parents—my grandmother, mother, and dad—or the fact that our dad was bipolar.

Not that having grandparents live with you is bad; in truth, it can be very good. There are lots of families who have in-law suites in their homes, or live-in grandparents. But the fact that we lived in my grandmother's house, and not she in ours, complicated things a bit—especially for my dad, who had learned as a child how to manipulate his mom to get whatever he wanted. Very few doctors, at least where we lived, understood the bipolar disorder at that time, and it was not diagnosed in my dad. This only added to the drama of thirty years of life with Grandma in our household, plus the remaining forty years after her passing.

Those first thirty years are what I remember as the silver years—not golden, but silver. Why silver? Because although silver is beautiful, it tarnishes easily. And that is how I would describe my growing up with Les: beautiful and exciting on one hand, but badly tarnished on the other. Whereas most children remember their mom more vividly in their growing-up years, my memories are dominated by the figure of my dad. That's probably because from my earliest recollection my grandmother and mother were always working, holding down the fort, bringing home the bacon.

They were the steady force in our family of five. Without them and the nine-to-five they put in every single day, we would not have had food on our table or a roof over our heads. They were the ones who taught my brother and me the importance of work. My dad, on the other hand, instilled in us the more passionate aspects of life, not so much by what he said, but by what he did and how he did it. This passion for life was a gift passed down in turn to our children. Elliot's graveside remarks reflected these memories.

"Our grandfather was the one who taught us how to drive a car and draw a cartoon," he continued. "He taught us how to hit a baseball. He told us funny jokes and riddles, and tickled us endlessly as we lay on the floor begging for more. He taught us to look into the heavens and see the stories of the stars, and to listen to the melody of a well-played song. He was the one who came to our basketball games and recitals and graduations."

That is how my son remembered it, but I don't remember Dad coming to *my* basketball games and recitals. When he did come, he was late; and my sharpest memory of him attending a graduation was the one he walked out of because he didn't like the speaker's liberal ideas. That was my brother's graduation, and it was during the time of the Vietnam War. The anti-war, anti-American remarks of the guest speaker did not sit well with my very patriotic World War II veteran dad.

Neither did my brother's long hair, which really wasn't long at all, but long enough to spark countless arguments and even all-out wars on many an afternoon when he and my dad tangled after school. How sad that something so trivial caused such hostility between these two men in my life! Steve wanted long sideburns like most of the musicians he idolized in the '70s, but Dad insisted he keep them an inch higher than his earlobe and took it as a personal affront that Steve refused to do so. I remember standing in the living room, crying quietly in the corner, while my dad pulled out his belt and forced Steve to choose between a belt lash and his sideburns. Steve chose his burns. Dad got his way in the end, though, and Steve got his hair cut.

My dad had mellowed quite a bit by the time the grandchildren came along. The things that had mattered most to him as the father of a teenager seemed to dissipate in light of what was really important in the big scheme of things. He no longer argued about hair length or Elvis Presley's gyrating pelvis. He didn't even yell at the Communists on television who were ruining our country—at least, not in front of the kids. Grandchildren had come along, and he had learned to adapt. He loved his grandkids, and made every attempt to be a part of all aspects of their lives. This was the experience of my son, which he fondly remembered.

"I think we can all agree," Elliot went on, "that there were both positives and negatives to our grandfather. As has already been so beautifully portrayed in the funeral remarks by my cousin, the life of Les Wilson was full of mistakes as well as love, honor, and blessing. Everyone gathered here today, especially our grandmother, is aware of the many mistakes my grandfather made. I guess you can't live 95 years without making lots of mistakes. But when I think about my grandfather's life and how I remember him best, one thought comes to mind. I recall more than anything that he was always there. That is what I remember most." My son wiped a tear from his eye. "He was always around! Papa was always there."

This I can attest. My dad really was always there. In fact, that was his legacy of blessing and curse to both my brother and me. My brother would not remember him being around as much as I did; I came six years later, and by that time my dad had stopped most of his all-night dancing and weekend road trips. I remember him being there every morning, still asleep, when I left for school; and every afternoon when I came home from school, he was there still, sitting in the brown leather recliner, reading the paper. His day always started around two in the afternoon.

There were different seasons of jobs in Dad's life. When he was selling something with his best friend and sidekick, Tommy P., he would shave and glue on his toupee. But when these sales jobs proved unprofitable, as they inevitably did, he slowly settled into becoming the maintenance man for the two apartment buildings Grandma had left us upon her death. This was the father I remember coming home to every day after school: an unshaven, unkempt man in an army green garage overall, with a large wrench in one hand and a toilet plunger in the other. By the time my brother had graduated college and moved out to the West Coast to pursue a music career, Les Wilson had become the custodian of our home.

My son shifted from one foot to the other as he glanced at each member of his family nearby. "I guess I will conclude by saying that Papa's legacy was one of love. He was always there because he loved us so much. He wanted so badly to achieve great wealth, so he could pass an inheritance down to each of us. We all know, of course, that he died with nothing in the way of monetary value. But what he gave us was something greater: himself. And because he gave us himself, we have countless stories and memories, gifts of the soul, to enjoy and pass down to our children. Papa was such a character…his spirit will be with us forever."

And I would have to agree. For in his death Dad had attained what he could never attain while living. He had become the center of our attention. Not forced or manipulated, for we were no longer dragged into the living room to be unwillingly chained to his presence in order to hear his lectures or advice. Instead, we now gathered together to retell every story we could summon to remembrance, laughing and crying at the memory of the life we both loved and hated, our life with the man we called Dad, Daddy, Papa, and Les.

MY EARLIEST MEMORY

"Daddy, Daddy, please don't go!" I yelled at the top of my lungs as I ran barefoot up the street after my dad.

He was walking quickly in long, angry, authoritative strides, gripping a large duffle bag that swung at his side. I was six years old. This is one of my earliest memories, and only one of many that haunt the darkness of my dreams of remembrance.

"Daddy, please wait! Please stop!" I finally caught up with him and tore at his pants as I clutched his leg, falling to my knees. He dragged me a bit before turning to tell me sharply to go home. "No, Daddy! Please! We didn't mean it!"

I really didn't know who hadn't meant what. I only knew somebody had said or done something to make him so mad that he was leaving us, and I knew that I didn't mean it, or they didn't mean it, whoever or whatever it was. None of us wanted him to leave.

Holding on to his leg with one arm, I reached with the other arm to grab at his jacket; crying bloody murder and begging him to stay, tears streaming down my cheeks, not sure if I might indeed fall victim to his rage. I can't say I ever really feared that, as my dad never physically abused my mother or me, although he did give my brother some pretty severe thrashings with a belt. His abuse was always more verbal and manipulative. And maybe this dramatic act of desertion was a form of manipulation as well, a method of getting his way. I didn't understand that at the time; all I knew was that my dad was leaving us, and I had to stop him.

"Don't leave me! Please don't leave me!" This time I was not the one crying out for mercy.

Almost fifty years had gone by, and now it was my dad who was pleading with me not to leave him. I stared at his frail and feeble body, pitifully curled in a fetal position on the plastic-coated hospital bed at the rehab center.

"I don't want to be left alone. You don't know what it's like here. They kidnapped me, and I couldn't escape!" he exclaimed, wild-eyed.

He proceeded to tell me how the rehab center had two sections: the good section (the one we were in), and the bad section, to which they had supposedly taken him by kidnapping and where they had kept him forcibly confined. He couldn't quite tell me what they had done to him that was so bad, but in his mind it was horrific, and he never wanted to go back. Of course, it was not really horrific at all. The truth was, the staff and nurses at the rehab center were extremely good and kind to my dad, but he had become delusional in his last days. He was talking to someone we could not see, and was giving names to his fork and pillow as if they were his best friends.

It brought tears to my eyes to see him in such a pitiable state the Sunday morning I entered his room—the last

Sunday of his life. Teeth out, mouth drawn in, stubble covering his face, thin gray hair sprouting out of his ears and the sides of his head, which was covered with moles and age spots. How different he looked, lying helpless on this bed, from that day long ago when I had held tightly to his pant legs, begging him to stay. I had helped him come to his senses that day, and he had returned to our home. I helped him come to his senses that morning in the rehab center, too, tenderly explaining that the nurses had not kidnapped him at all but had simply taken him to therapy, where they were trying to help him.

"What do you say if I clean you up a bit?" I asked.

"Oh, that would be so nice." He gave me a big toothless grin.

So I shaved him, trimmed his ear hair and eyebrows, and cleaned his food-covered denture as best as I could. I washed and combed his hair, and told him how handsome he looked.

"You know something?" he said.

"What?" I asked.

"You are beautiful," he declared with a twinkle in his eye. "You are really beautiful!"

My eyes began to fill with water. I think that was the first time he had ever said I was beautiful. It wasn't that he was loath to pay a compliment; it's just that he had never paid me one like that before. Little did I know it would be the last compliment he would ever give me. All my life I had wanted to hear that I was beautiful to my dad. He had told me I looked nice. He had told me I was funny and clever and smart. But he had never told me I was beautiful.

What is it about that word that makes such a difference to a young girl—or, in my case, a not-so-young girl? Was it just me, or do most girls long to hear their dads say they are beautiful? I had grown up in the shadow of a very beautiful mom, and in the shadow of dozens of bigger-than-life, silver-screen women whose beauty was always talked about as if that was what made them significant. My dad had the eye of an artist, and he looked at beauty with calculated perception. Sometimes I felt as if my statistics did not calculate according to my dad's expectations.

Growing up long and lean, I didn't really get a figure until high school. When I did start to mature physically, I remember my dad noticing, and telling me I had pretty legs. I took that one to the bank, and never forgot it. So if I say I will never forget the compliment my dad made to me in the rehab center, I will not. It meant something to me that after fifty-plus years, my dad had finally told his only daughter that she was beautiful.

All my life I had tried to please my dad—and that was not an easy thing to do. Good was never good enough.

The goals I felt my dad had set for me were too high and unattainable. Whether it was really he who had set those goals, or whether they had been cast up by my own imagination and attributed to him, I do not know. I only know that I felt I was never what he wanted or had hoped for in a daughter.

It seemed that no matter how hard I tried, I could not measure up. I was too loud. I was too clumsy. I never felt pretty enough. I wasn't graceful enough. Of course, what thirteen-year-old girl is? Even when I reached young adulthood, however, and the rest of my body caught up with my legs, I still never thought I was good enough for my dad. I knew he loved me, and he tried to encourage and support me in his own way. It wasn't that he never complimented me; it was just that almost every compliment had a "but" to it, and it was those "buts" that always made me feel like I missed the mark.

"You have a pleasant voice, but…" "Your essay is good, but…" "Your speech is engaging, but…" "You look pretty, but…" Of course, there were also the outright criticisms: "Why did you go and cut your hair?" "That outfit is *not* very becoming." "What kind of music is *that*?" "Where did you pick up *those* friends?" As we watched old movies together, it became obvious to me that what he really wanted in a daughter was a film star. "Just look at Rita Hayworth. What beauty! What grace!" I longed for him to say those things to me.

So it was especially nice on that Sunday morning, the last Sunday I saw my dad alive, that he gave me an unqualified, genuine compliment. I was beautiful to him, maybe for the first time in his life. Fifty years of pent-up emotion swelled in my throat. If only he could have told me this fifty years earlier I might have felt better about myself as a teenager and young adult. Not that I wanted to blame him for my perceptions. I knew better than to blame my parents for my personal demons or life choices, but I wondered if I might have seen myself and my place in the world differently. As I thought about what could have been, in contrast to what was, an overwhelming sadness flooded my soul. Dad didn't notice the tear sliding down my cheek. He had already fallen back to sleep.

He slept more than usual the last few days of his life. And that is saying something, because sleep had always been one of my dad's favorite pastimes. Actually, it was the saving grace for the emotional suffering caused by his bipolar depression. At the very least, it seemed to calm the tumultuous storms of my dad's rollercoaster behavior, and gave the rest of us some much-needed peace. After he blew up, sending us all scrambling for cover from the shotgun of his angry tirades, he would enter his sanctuary—the middle room of our row house apartment—and fall into a double bed squeezed between two dressers and a built-out closet he had constructed years earlier.

He would sleep for a couple of hours, awake to tell us he was sorry, and act as if nothing had happened. Then he would sit down to sketch out on paper a new idea for a project he was working on, or make his way to the garage he had built as a workshop to construct his many inventions.

As a little girl, I could not put it all together. But as I got older, I began to see a pattern: once a month my dad would cycle, and all hell would break loose. We would have two weeks of happy, and then BAM! There was no rhyme or reason to what would set him off. Maybe someone didn't squeeze the toothpaste right. Maybe my brother didn't wash the car. Maybe my grandmother didn't give him as much money as he wanted. Maybe my mom didn't get him dinner quickly enough. I wasn't usually the one to make him go off; I was the peacemaker. It was always the women who ganged up on him, and the son who rebelled. It's funny how things turn out: when we got older, I became the one who rebelled, and my brother became the conciliator. But for twenty-three years, until I married, I was the one who kept the peace, or tried to.

"No, Daddy! Please don't!" I begged, as I watched him rip his belt out of the loops of his pants.

My brother had done something and was about to get a beating. Another memory from the recesses of my mind. I don't remember what he did, only that it wasn't worthy of the belt, nor of my dad's fierce anger.

"Leave the room, Audrey!" my dad commanded sternly.

"No, Daddy! He didn't mean it!" I pleaded.

Seems like that was my "go to" answer: whoever it was, they "didn't mean it." I didn't mean to leave the cap off the milk. Grandma didn't mean to put down your ideas. Momma didn't mean to side with Grandma. Steve didn't mean to do whatever it was he did. I didn't care what Steve had done, I just knew I loved my brother and didn't want to see him get this beating. I thought I was pleading for his life. Although my pleading did not prevent the lashings, I think it kept Dad from giving my brother as many as he would have otherwise.

Yes, I was the peacemaker, and my dad knew it. After he had made everyone's day unbearable, especially his own, he would come to my bedroom, get on his knees beside my bed, and start crying. The older he got the more routine this became, and the more copious his tears. He knew when he had behaved badly. It was during these times that our roles were reversed, and he would do the begging—begging for my forgiveness. It was my forgiveness he wanted, even if I wasn't the one he had hurt. It was important to him to be loved and forgiven. And of course, it was important that we forgive. I did forgive, but sometimes I would think terrible thoughts. Sometimes I wished he would just go away and never come back, or even die.

One night in particular stands out in my mind. I was in middle school. My dad blew up over something, and unleashed his anger on the first person he saw. Being the only one home that evening, I was the recipient of his explosive rage. I had nothing to do with whatever it was that had gone wrong; I don't even remember what it was, although it most likely had to do with money. But he needed someone to blame, and I was the one he used as his verbal punching bag. It was the first time I had faced my dad's emotional demons all alone, but it would not be the last.

I stood there and took it without a word—unlike my brother, who would have given it right back. I think my silence made it worse, at least for me. The verbal assault continued for what seemed like an eternity before he ran out of words and steam. He finally dismissed me, and I flew to my room like a bat out of hell. I slammed the door, hoping he heard me but at the same time scared that if he did I might get a physical whipping to match the verbal one.

I fell on my bed face down and hugged my pillow tightly. I remember clenching my fists and hitting my pillow over and over. I kept repeating aloud, in a quiet voice, that I hated him and wanted him to die. I even envisioned a knife in my hand. I could not get the awful picture of me stabbing him out of my mind. I wrestled with these horrible thoughts for hours before his sheepish frame appeared in my doorway.

All it took was one look at his pitiful face and I knew I had to forgive him. He fell on his knees beside my bed and put his hand in mine. He kept repeating how sorry he was, and begged my forgiveness, not realizing I had already given it. I pulled him close and hugged his neck, feeling his wet tears against my cheek. I told him it was okay. He told me over and over and over how sorry he was, and that it would never happen again. But I knew it would. I also knew that I would always forgive him. How could I not? He was my dad and I loved him; and I saw in him a great deal of good to compensate for the bad. Yes, there were cycles of pain—much pain; but in between there was great beauty.

A BEAUTIFUL MIND

My dad was almost too intelligent and gifted for his own good. He could never corral his thoughts; they shot out of his brain like electrodes on steroids.

He not only thought beautiful thoughts, but painted them as well. My favorite was the painting of the elephant with three legs. My brother's favorite was the wagon with three wheels. My father's perfectionism, coupled with his bipolar disease, never allowed him to finish anything. Not a painting. Not a project. Not any piece of work. He never held down a job for very long, and was always "self-employed."

There were pluses and minuses to this way of life. The negative was that there was never enough money. The positive was that he had a lot of time on his hands, time to teach my brother and me some really neat things. He taught me how to draw, for instance, and later on his grandchildren, too. My nephew, Jack, ran with it and became a wonderful artist.

Dad was brilliant. He was creative. He was a talented singer and actor, had the mind of an architect, and the imagination of an artist. He was also friendly and likable. Only his family knew the darker side of this very gifted man. If only he could have harnessed these gifts, he could have used them to accomplish something in which he felt purpose. If only someone could have guided or mentored him! If only they had been able to diagnose the bipolar disorder, so that he could have received treatment and help! There are lots of "if only's"; there are always "if only's"… but you cannot live in regret; you cannot change the past. Still, you wonder what might have happened differently—"if only."

A beautiful mind generates lots of ideas, and my dad was full of them. In fact, during his manic phases, which lasted weeks, he would produce so many ideas that neither we nor he could keep up with them all. His mind raced from one project to the next. He would start a project in the living room, only to leave it half-finished and start another one in the kitchen. He would leave that one unfinished, so that he could begin a new project in the garage. Our home, yard, garage, and basement were constantly filled with unfinished projects. When the two-week manic episode was over, the projects would sit idly by, waiting for their creator to return and complete them. Sometimes he would get back to working on them; sometimes not. Most of the time, it was left to our grandmother to either finish the task or clean it up. And as Steve and I got older, it was left to us.

Some of the projects were designed with us in mind. The miniature golf course was one such creation. I remember it well, because my brother and I spent our entire summer sifting dirt all day for our dad. Dad had made several different-sized filters for just this purpose, using old window screens salvaged from our apartments. The series of sifters eventually converted large particles into very minute ones by means of a process similar to that used by the Forty-Niners. Why he didn't just purchase a truckload of fine sand is beyond me, but at the time I was too young to ask questions.

He constructed two par-three miniature golf holes onto which he poured our grainy gold. After leveling the fine dirt to perfection, he planted grass seed on top, envisioning a true putting green. Most of the grass did not grow, however, and what little did grow was washed away with the first rain. All our hard work was washed away as well; my dad became bored with the project and moved on to something else. Although disappointed that we wouldn't get to be the envy of every kid in the neighborhood, we were secretly glad the project was over; our summer was drawing to a close, and we wanted to do something with it besides turn dirt into sand. My brother celebrated by taking me to a real miniature golf course and beating me by ten strokes.

The architecturally designed train track that expanded to fill our entire attic was another project, which brought great joy to my brother and dad. Dad designed and painted every wee building, which included a local fire station and post office. He meticulously placed each blade of grass personally, and with great precision and forethought arranged every piece of foliage surrounding his little town of carefully crafted bungalows. I was a little too preoccupied with boys by that time to care much about it; but I do remember my dad showing me, with great pride, the detailed construction of his little railroad town. I also remember it being unfinished and staying that way till we moved away and left it lying in the attic.

He invented other things as well, such as wooden stick games to keep me occupied when I was bored. He turned our basement into a club for my brother and his music buddies, and then invented an intercom system to keep an eye (or ear) on them. Steve did most of the work on this project, with Dad supervising from a distance. Although my dad was not a drinker, and did not allow alcohol in our home, he made a bar setting for the hangout, complete with pool table and black lighting, very popular in that day.

The three-story electric Christmas tree was probably my favorite invention. Long before Christmas decorations became electronic sculptures of light, movement, and brilliance, my dad designed and built a forty-foot wooden Christmas tree, complete with synchronized lighting sequences that danced in rainbow colors to Christmas music played through a loudspeaker off our front porch. He did finish the tree—but the kicker is, he finished it after Christmas. We didn't get the tree up till New Year's Eve.

Needless to say, we missed the Citywide Christmas Light Contest my dad wanted to win. We still summoned all the neighbors and tenants to help, hoisting the tree up with rope and pulley from the attic window of our apartment building. I remember I was the only one small enough to actually crawl through the window and sit on the ledge overhanging the attic. I had the responsibility of guiding the rope as my brother stood behind me and pulled. Everyone else was on the ground thirty feet below, raising the tree, like neighbors at an Amish barn-raising. The tree stayed up till right before Easter.

Those were the beautiful moments. There were many of them, sandwiched between mood swings and irrational outbreaks. Those beautiful moments were the highs of the bipolar mindset; the lows were a different story. And sleep was a welcome guest for my dad when the lows came to town.

SO LONELY

"Wake up, Dad," I whispered quietly as I nudged his shoulder. "I'm here. Time to get up."

It was early Sunday morning, and I had just arrived to sit with him at the rehab center while my mom and brother took a much-needed break. He woke up startled and not quite aware of his surroundings. Then he saw me, and remembered where he was. He began weeping.

"I've been waiting all night for you to come."

"I'm here, Daddy."

"Where have you *been*? I've been so lonely!"

His words came out broken, laden with anguish. At the sound of his barely audible voice, the bitter walls of resentiment I had built around my heart began to crumble. He was weak and tired and frail, and probably dying. At the time, I did not realize how close to death he actually was.

"Where is Gen?" he asked. "Why didn't she stay with me last night?"

"Mom is back at the house getting some rest," I explained patiently. "She was here all day yesterday until closing time. She has been here eight or ten hours every day, sitting in this chair right beside your bed. The doctor said if she doesn't get her rest, she's not going to be with us much longer. When Steve gets home from church he's going to bring her. I'm going to stay with you till she gets here."

"I don't like being by myself."

That was no overstatement. He never liked being alone. He would rather I stay up late with him listening to music or watching television, and miss school the next day, than be an "A" student. Amazingly enough, I was an "A" student nonetheless, and I think it was because I so badly wanted to please him.

I cannot remember him doing anything by himself. He wouldn't even run his errands alone. I always dreaded him saying, "Come go with me," because I knew that meant spending several tedious hours on countless errands. This continued for years; in fact, that particular trait of my dad's was remembered by all the grandkids the day after we buried him, as we gathered around to tell "Papa" stories. It made us laugh then. My nephew Jack recalled numerous times when his grandfather would pick him up after school, forcing him to ride shotgun as he drove from store to store taking care of business—business he could easily have taken care of beforehand. But that was not his way; he waited on purpose till school was over, because he wanted Jack with him.

Jack was the youngest of the cousins, my brother Steve's only son—a miracle baby born to him and his wife Angie late in life. He was the only child they were able to have, and was a blessing to us all. To Jack's credit, he enjoyed his time with his Pop. It was a sweet thing to see how patient and understanding Jack was, and what great buddies he and his grandfather were, and it was an even sweeter thing to hear him share the memory.

Dad did not like working alone, either. He did not like eating alone. He did not like traveling alone. He did not like doing *anything* alone, except one thing, and that was sleeping. When he got older, he didn't even like doing that alone. Mom had to be by his side before he fell asleep, and had to stay there in the event he awoke in the middle of the night. Needless to say, this new arrangement, where Mom was actually going home to get some rest, did not sit well with him.

"And they turned off the light," he continued, as he struggled to explain to me the anxiety he felt at being left alone. "You know I don't like being in the dark! Why can't you take turns staying with me?" he implored.

"Dad," I addressed him tenderly but firmly. "First of all, Steve has to be with Angie. She has been sick for the past six months, and Steve hasn't even been able to go to work."

Angie had been suffering with terrible pain in her neck and ears. She had been off work herself for the past seven months and had been put through all kinds of tests, MRIs, and CAT scans, as well as two major surgeries on her neck and ears. The doctors finally concluded it was some form of a rare nerve disease, one of the results being hardening of scar tissue, which led to further pain and migraines. I concluded it was a result of accumulated stress from the fact that my dad had lived with them for the past twenty years.

I tried to reason with Dad. "Steve has been under a lot of pressure trying to take care of Angie…and I don't even live here. I haven't been home in over two weeks! Besides, visitors have to leave at eight; there's no place for us to stay. You do realize you are the only patient here who has someone stay with him every day all day long, don't you? Most of the other patients only get visitors on the weekends."

"I know," he said sweetly.

He actually seemed to get it. There were times he was really a dad, and then there were other times he was more like a child. Most people would say that was normal for an aging parent, but my dad had been like this all my life. Age had little to do with it fifty years ago; it was just who he was. Age did nothing but magnify an already dysfunctional personality.

"I know you're doing your best," he added. "I know you can't be here all the time. I have the best family!" He started to cry. "God has given me the best family. I thank Him every day for my family. I know I have the best wife. She is so strong; I am not. She amazes me. She can run circles around me!"

He knew he had married an angel; my mom had been his faithful companion and servant for the past seventy-two years. She really was amazing! Although I was almost forty years younger, she ran circles around me as well. I prayed I could be as good a mom and as faithful a wife as she had been, but I feared I had too much of my dad in me to live up to that expectation. I was no Gen Ash. I was more like my dad.

Not that that was such a bad thing, all told. There were lots of qualities about my dad that I cherished. But I fear that both my brother and I inherited some of the bipolar disorder ourselves—if not in our bodies, then as a result of the environment that shaped our experience and outlook on life. Bipolar disorder was the air we breathed. Looking back over my brother's life I can see how it affected him in his early teens and young adult years. He battled it, and received treatment and medication, which helped him tremendously. He also learned the healing power of forgiveness; that, along with all the other parts of his spiritual journey, matured him into a man of abundant kindness, patience, and generosity.

It did not show up in me until later in life, after my kids were grown and gone. I had serious and lengthy bouts with despair and depression that cycled much like my dad's temper. Whereas Steve's bipolar waves expressed themselves in fits of anger, mine manifested as analytical self-destruction and self-depreciation. The "sins of the fathers" are indeed passed down to the children, it seems—not that they have to be, but it takes a small miracle to stop the cycle, both within and without.

Interestingly enough, only those who knew me best were even aware that I suffered. My husband knew. My children saw it, but probably couldn't figure it out. One close friend knew more toward the end, when I couldn't hold it in any longer. For the most part, though, everyone thought I lived a life of comfort and luxury: great husband, great kids, great house, every possible need realized and met. I even fooled everyone at church, as I continued all my ministry and mission responsibilities with unabated efficiency and perfection.

I finally got tired of pretending to be perfect, and took a break from all my service projects. I needed some time to sort things out. I needed to figure out what was going on inside me that made me feel so worthless, so "less than" everyone else. The secrets of my past started to resurface, and were enough to send me into the dark places of my mind. That, coupled with some serious conflicts in the thirtieth year of my marriage, was enough to keep me in those dark places for a very long time. Eventually I started writing as a way of dealing with the pain and trying to figure out the solution. When, on top of all that, my dad passed away, I needed time to grieve and reflect on his role in my life. The best way I knew to do that was to put it on paper.

But that came after April 23, 2015. Today was only April 20, and I was standing in front of the sad and feeble man I called my father. As I stood there, I thought about my growing-up years, what they had meant to me, and how it had come down to this, and I started crying too. I hadn't cried for a long time over my dad. I had learned to ignore his complaints, or simply walk out of the room; many times I walked right out of the house.

There was one Saturday morning I did just that, and but for the grace of God it might have been the last time I walked out on anyone. As was so often the case, the argument was over something trivial, something I no longer remember. What I do remember was that I had reached a breaking point. I recall him saying, as he had said countless other times, "Children are to be seen and not heard." I must have angered him by intervening on Mom's behalf; I knew that children should not interfere in their parents' business, that things beyond our awareness or understanding happened behind closed doors.

I cycled too, between stoic restraint and blowing up. I would go weeks patiently ignoring the criticisms and negative comments Dad made to my mom, and the way he gave orders to her like a master commanding a slave. I said nothing, figuring she had made her choice and it was her business. But my indignation would build and build until something was said or done that made me snap. After a while, the years of sitting idly by and saying nothing were over, and then I cycled back and forth between playing peacemaker and acting as district attorney and judge. On this particular Saturday, I'd had enough of the peacemaker role and made myself prosecutor, judge, and jury. I knew my cause was righteous, and I hung my dad out to dry.

If my intent had been to get my dad to stop abusing my mom, then my method worked, because he switched his focus from her to me. But instead of allowing him to shred my personhood as he had hers, I simply walked out of the house. When he demanded I come back, I ignored him and got into my car. He followed me outside and watched as I backed out of the driveway. He yelled for me to come back, but I just shook my head and kept going, not sure where I was headed but determined to get away. He kept hollering for me to return, so I rolled the window up to block him out, and rolled up a different kind of window in my heart to block out the pain.

I kept driving till I got to Sardis, Mississippi. My brother had taken me to that spot many a Saturday when we were younger and he was looking for girls. Sardis was a man-made beach that boasted booze and bikinis; Steve didn't care for the booze, but he loved the bikinis. It was the only place I could think to go where I could hang out all day and be by myself.

I lay on the beach in my street clothes and thought about my dad. At one point I decided it best not to think at all; I closed my eyes and fell asleep. When I woke up it was starting to get dark, and I knew I needed to head back home. As crazy as home was, it was where I belonged, and where I knew I was loved. Dad really did love me. He wanted me to stay close by and never leave home, ever; he had tried to talk me into going to Memphis State University, as Steve had done, but I had made my way to an out-of-town college as soon as I graduated from high school. And now I was out of town again, and it was late, and I knew it was time to go home.

I picked up what few belongings I had with me and began walking back to my little orange Honda Civic. As I started home it began to drizzle—a fitting end to a gloomy day. I was halfway home when my car began to sputter and stall, slowing down without my help. I pressed on the accelerator to try to speed up, but to no avail. I finally pulled over onto the shoulder to wait out the rain; this had happened once before, and I knew that if I just let the car sit awhile, and the rain die down, then I could probably get it started again without calling my dad. And I did not want to call my dad.

As I sat there, a sense of foreboding came over me. I looked up, and saw to my left a man standing outside my window. I hid my initial reaction of fear quite well and smiled to relieve the tension, but I knew better than to roll down my window. He kept talking loudly and motioning for me to open the car door. I cracked the window just enough to hear what he had to say, and he told me that he wanted to help me, that I should get into his car with him. He could take me to a dry place and get me some help for my car. I thanked him, but told him that wasn't necessary.

He didn't look evil. He looked like an average guy in his late twenties or early thirties. There was nothing particularly memorable about him—except his persistence. He kept insisting I get out of my car and into his; at one point he even tried to push his hand through the cracked-open window, but the opening was too small for him to get his whole hand in. I knew then that I needed to get out of there as quickly as possible. My heart was racing, but I did not want him to know I was afraid; so I smiled and thanked him for his help while nonchalantly turning the key in the ignition. The engine would not turn over. He got a little more agitated; I got a little more scared. I tried again, and the engine still didn't turn over. I was shaking now, but I knew I had to hold it together if I was going to get out of there alive. I whispered a prayer as I tried a third time. The engine cranked up, and I sped away, leaving the strange man behind in the rain.

As I pulled onto the interstate, I glanced toward heaven and thanked God for helping me. I realized I could have been talking to a serial killer who saw me as his next victim. Whether he was really a killer or not I will never know, but I do know he wanted something I wasn't willing to give. I also know I would never have ended up in that predicament if I hadn't gotten so angry and stormed off. How foolish of me to put myself in jeopardy because of an argument with my dad! To this day, I believe that had it not been for my guardian angel, the next time anyone saw me might have been on the back of a milk carton.

I was glad to get home. By then Dad had calmed down, and it was as if nothing had happened; he didn't ask about my day, and I didn't tell him. I kept the roadside incident to myself, as I did a lot of things back then. I had learned how to keep secrets, and neither my mother or father knew just how scared I was, or how fortunate I felt to be alive. As I lay on my bed that night, a tear of relief slid down onto my pillow.

And years later, as I stood in front of my elderly father, the tears continued to pour down my cheeks. I thought about all the good times we had shared, and the bad. As I stared at the cream-colored concrete wall behind his bed, I stared into my own soul. Like my dying father, I too felt alone. I had built up walls of isolation, and the hidden feelings of bitterness, anger, shame, and sadness that lay behind those walls had festered into an undetectable infection.

THE WALLS

Wall building had become easy for me—almost second nature. I don't think I was even aware of it at the time. Recently I had built a wall between my own emotions and serving my dad's needs: I wasn't going to let my emotions breach the barrier that kept me sane. My brother Steve, the one-time rebel who had now matured into the peacemaker, noticed.

"Audrey, you are too hard," he said firmly but kindly as we sat around the dinner table at his house in Nashville, trying to figure out what to do with our dad. "I'm telling you this for your own good. You have to forgive."

At first I resented him for telling me that. Had I not been forgiving Dad my whole life? And who was Steve to tell me I had to forgive, when, most of the time, defending him or my mom was the very reason I had gotten into a verbal war with my dad in the first place? It wasn't for my own benefit that I was telling my dad the harsh truth; it was to help *them*. Had living with my dad all these years blinded my brother to my dad's manipulative ways, as it had blinded my mom?

Maybe he was right; maybe I was being too harsh. After all, my dad was ninety-five years old. But couldn't Steve see how self-centered Dad was? Surely Dad realized that my ninety-two-year-old mom could no longer wait on him hand and foot without it taking a toll on her ninety-five-pound body. After Steve's urgent call the day before, hadn't I driven three hours to come and take care of Dad on hearing that Mom had fallen while trying to help him? Was no one getting it? My dad was still asking my mom to fry him an egg just thirty minutes after her fall to the ground! And after she'd been at the doctor's all day getting her hip x-rayed, my dad was still waking her up in the middle of the night to ask her for a drink!

Did no one but me see the selfishness of this man, and was I the only one who was going to say something? I guess my brother had grown accustomed to my dad's ways, much as Professor Higgins had grown accustomed to Eliza's face. In truth, he'd had plenty of time to do so, having taken my parents in when they could no longer afford to pay rent on a house, and given them a place to live in a side apartment he built especially for the purpose. For more than twenty years Steve had provided for my parents, with help from me when needed. Mom still had her social security check, which they lived on, but without Steve my parents would have been without a roof over their heads.

How life changes things! I remember the day I was telling my brother that *he* had to forgive. I remember the days when I would get between my brother and my dad to keep them from killing each other. No longer a little girl, I had grown big enough by then to think I could somehow prevent two grown men from tearing each other's throats out. Steve was a grown man, and yet my dad still tried to run his life. This caused countless arguments, some of which led to knock-down drag-out fights with fists put through walls; it is to their credit that they hit the walls and not each other's faces. I was usually the one who patched the walls, and I was also the one who tried to patch the relationship.

The problem was, I had a big hole in my own heart that needed patching, and I never figured that out until after my dad's death. The hole first appeared when I was six, the day I chased my dad up the street begging him to return. It got a little bigger every time my dad had a manic-depressive cycle and blew up—every time he broke something in anger, or threatened to leave if we didn't straighten up. With every abusive word, every degrading remark, every accusing finger and thoughtless action from Dad, the hole inside me grew. As a child I didn't understand the dangers associated with an unhealthy heart; I later learned the hard way. It took a long time to figure that out, and it took a long time to patch up the hole.

I had grown up as a child who never questioned her elders and always complied with their demands. This, coupled with the feeling of not measuring up to my father's expectations, laid the groundwork for some painful experiences. I never wanted to talk about them. They were secrets I kept hidden.

Eventually I would open that closet, but only after my heart was broken many times; it took that kind of demolition to tear down the walls I had built up. It would be a while before I could dig out from under the rubble of my hurts and shameful past and be whole again. I had seen and heard and felt too much, had filled the hole inside me with concrete and let it harden. I had watched my dad manipulate my grandmother, mother, and brother all my life, had sat by and observed as he belittled his beautiful, hardworking wife and devoted son, and made no defense for them except "They didn't mean it."

My mom and brother had performed countless seemingly unappreciated acts of service for my dad, especially in the latter years of his life. Steve would take him on road trips and train rides, play poker and dominoes with him, and make sure he had plenty of old movies and music to entertain him, yet nothing seemed to satisfy Dad. My family did things for him as well, and while he did express appreciation at times, it seemed he was always complaining or pouting about something. And in the last year of his life, my mom had been chained to him constantly, tending to every need, from serving food on his lap at all hours of the night to changing his paper briefs (he could no longer make it to the toilet in time), to washing, dressing, and grooming him. In the latter years he seemed to mellow, having lost the energy to fight his demons outwardly; but those demons remained, and still made him unbearable to be around much of the time. Mom continued to be his servant with little time left in the day to be a wife.

That is really what made me bitter toward my dad, so that I said some hard things to him when I was old enough to have the courage to speak out. I was especially bitter that he had been so irresponsible all his life. My mother and grandmother had been the providers, while my dad pretty much did whatever he wanted whenever he wanted to do it. Because he never felt the responsibility for providing, he'd had the freedom to pursue his own ambitions, lucrative or not. And pursue them he did.

THE ENTERPRISES

After my dad passed away, I spent a lot of time reminiscing about him with Mom and asking her tons of questions. I found out quite a few things that made me feel sad for my dad. He had on several occasions genuinely attempted to make a living and provide for his family. He tried his hand at lots of different things, some of which I know firsthand because I was old enough to see them for myself, and some of which I can only pass down as they were told to me.

The tire shop was one such business adventure that was typical of my dad's so-called luck. He borrowed money from my Uncle Jordan, who was an incredibly sharp businessman. Uncle Jordan was my grandmother's brother, and the most successful of all my dad's relatives; if you could get him on board, then you pretty much had it made. At the encouragement of my grandmother, Uncle Jordan had given my dad the funds needed to start the tire shop.

Dad worked hard preparing the shop and stocking it with supplies, equipment, and, of course, lots of tires. The one thing he did not think about was insurance. It is my understanding that Uncle Jordan instructed him to get insurance, but Dad waited till it was too late. Before he got around to looking into it, something caught fire in the shop and the whole building burned to the ground, destroying all the equipment, supplies, and tires, as well as Uncle Jordan's faith in my dad. Devastated, my father went home and went to bed.

That faith was rekindled, however, when my dad became involved in a company called Nutrilite. Dad made a considerable effort to build his personal organization in this fast-growing multilevel company, which produced quality vitamin supplements. Nutrilite was the first multilevel marketing business that my dad invested in; there would be many more, but none as successful as Nutrilite. He had hundreds of investors (called distributors) signed up under him, one of whom was Uncle Jordan.

My dad actually had in his possession (my mom now has it) a copy of a signed check from Elvis Presley, who purchased a year's supply of Nutrilite product from Uncle Jordan. I remember my dad saying that both Elvis and the famous actor Nick Adams were part of his downline; whether they were actual distributors I am not certain, but I know that Vernon Presley, Elvis's dad and a personal friend of my great-uncle's, purchased the products from my great-uncle and had them mailed overseas to Germany where Elvis was stationed during the war.

Dad worked very hard building his organization with meetings, trips, and incentives. He was actually doing very well and bringing in quite an income until the thing that sometimes happens with such companies happened: the three partners who started the business had a falling out and split up, taking their money and going their separate ways. The company came to an end, leaving unemployed all the people who had been under the partners. Dad's organization fell apart, and once again he was devastated. The smarter members regrouped and started Amway; my dad, on the other hand, went home and went to bed.

Dad would tell you that had it not been for the communists, the timberland he bought in Brazil would have made him a wealthy man. He would also tell you that his oil well in Texas should have made him rich, but he and his five friends got cheated by the Texans, who sold him a gusher that had already gushed. Les was always looking for that big deal that would bring him his pot of gold. The problem was that the pot usually turned out to be filled with mush—at least, that's what my dad would tell you.

My dad would also tell you that his medical discharge from the service was a piece of bad luck. His medical exam indicated he had tuberculosis; later, after he was sent home, the spot on his lung disappeared. It was devastating to my dad at the time, because he loved the Air Corps where he served, and talked about it the rest of his life. I often tried to tell him that perhaps the discharge was God's way of watching out for him; after all, he could have been sent to Pearl Harbor or one of the hot spots in Europe. But Dad never saw it that way. He always saw it as an extension of his personal failure.

After his discharge from the service, he had an opportunity to pick up his education where he'd left off. He re-entered the university and resumed studying architecture, but quit a year short of graduation because someone came along and told him he could make a lot of money selling siding. It didn't take long for him to discover there was not much money in selling siding door to door, at least not in his case. But it didn't stop him from having many more such grandiose ideas, always starting his new businesses with Grandma's money and high hopes, only to have them bitterly dashed by some disappointing circumstance. He called it bad luck or being jinxed, and would retreat to his bed and stay there for days.

The business venture I remember best was the Mexican pot shop. I don't mean marijuana, although that might have been one business he could have succeeded at. I'm talking about ceramic pots made in Mexico and brought across the border. I remember this one well, because I was the "lucky" child who got to travel with him to Mexico to buy the merchandise. I'll never forget the two trips we made; the first almost landed us in jail, and the second almost landed us in the grave.

My brother and I both accompanied Dad on his first trip to Mexico. We bought hundreds of cheaply painted ceramic pots and pictures. Our Mexican pot shop stocked a hodgepodge of items, from wrought-iron plant stands to turquoise jewelry, to paintings on black velvet. Believe it or not, kitschy as they were, the black velvet paintings actually sold pretty well. The biggest sellers were the ones with Jesus on the cross or the Last Supper. But the most famous were the ones of Mickey Mouse and Donald Duck. They were popular…and they were illegal.

They were illegal because the Mexican painters weren't licensed to use the Disney characters, and therefore anyone who bought the pictures was subject to huge fines or time in a Mexican prison. My dad, who loved the works of Walt Disney, couldn't resist the pictures, and bought several dozen; when we crossed the border, the customs officer searched our trailer and almost threw Dad in jail. I think when they saw he had a little twelve-year-old girl in the truck with him, they let him off lightly, deciding just to seize the pictures and let us go.

The second trip was only my dad and me and even scarier than the first. Dad had purchased a truck to haul our merchandise back and forth from Mexico. At first everything was good; my dad always tried to make our road trips fun, and we played the "ABC" game, looking for letters in different road signs until one of us completed the entire alphabet. Even though Dad had to keep his eyes on the road, it was still hard to beat him. He was very competitive and hated losing. Another game we'd play was "Twenty

Questions," with Dad being the one who thought of a person—usually a movie star or important historical figure—and I the one who had to ask the yes-or-no questions. He also loved to play "Name that Tune," where I was supposed to guess the name of the song he was whistling. We played this game in the evening, when his mood tended to be more mellow; sunset was his favorite time of day and put him in a peaceful frame of mind. He never really enjoyed sunrise, but he loved it when the sun sank slowly over the horizon and the sky became a misty grey as the street lights began to appear.

My dad was not a morning person. Part of the reason for this was his lifestyle: in the early years Dad would stay out late dancing, and in the middle years he would stay up late watching the dancers. Fred Astaire and Ginger Rogers were his favorites. His usual bedtime was about two in the morning, and he'd wake up long after the rest of us had left for work and school. Interestingly enough, I inherited this body clock, and to this day I have a hard time going to sleep at night. Not a very healthy habit for an adult, but as a young teenager on a road trip with her dad, it had its perks.

We would drive through most of the night, taking turns at the wheel; he let me drive when I was twelve, having taught both my brother and me how to drive as soon as our feet could reach the pedals. He didn't care that there were laws about minimum driving age, as he believed the government was too invasive anyway, and he had the freedom to live his life his way as long as it didn't hurt anyone. Besides, both my brother and I were exceptional drivers. He was as strict and thorough as any certified driving instructor, taking us to unfinished freeways and teaching us how to shift gears and stop on a dime. We learned on a five-speed stick shift station wagon before graduating to an automatic sedan. He also taught us how to parallel-park a van and a truck, as well as change a tire and the oil. We learned all this by the age of twelve, so that we could help Dad out on road trips when needed.

Dad also taught us how to shoot. Steve claims Dad never taught him, but I remember well how Dad would line up cans on a picket fence out in the country and give me his pistol to shoot at them much like the metal ducks at the traveling carnival. With each success, he pulled me back a few more feet and let me try again. He also taught me how to point, aim, and shoot my brother's twenty-two rifle, which came in pretty handy for this particular trip to the Rio Grande. As it happened, we didn't have to shoot anyone, but it might have turned out differently if Dad hadn't had his thinking cap on.

The highway we were traveling was not a very well-traveled one, and there were long straight stretches with nothing visible but a few cacti growing in the open desert landscape on both sides. Gas stations and other signs of civilization were few and far between. We had traveled this road for about an hour, getting closer and closer to the Mexican border, when I began to notice my dad looking in the rearview mirror quite a bit. Turning around to see what he was looking at, I spotted a single car close behind us. I asked my dad about it, and he said there was nothing to worry about; he was just keeping an eye on the car because it had been behind us for a while.

I took my dad at his word and did not worry, until he asked me to reach behind him and pull the rifle out from under the back seat. I guess he could tell I was scared, as he tried to comfort me by telling me he was just taking precautions. The car had been following us for several hours now, slowing down or accelerating, matching our own speed. At one point it got close enough for me to see the two men occupying the front seat of the car. It was too dark inside the car for me to see facial features, but both the men had dark hair and what looked like mustaches. I couldn't make out much more than that, except that they looked seriously intent...and I was frightened.

I asked my dad if we were going to be okay, and if he was scared. He said yes to both questions. He thought the men were waiting for us to get into the deepest part of the desert, where they could make their move and rob us. Although he didn't say so, I suspected he was thinking they might do even worse than that to us. I believe my dad was especially concerned for my safety, as we had read about other travelers being robbed and killed, and young girls raped, close to the border. He tried to reassure me by telling me he had a plan; when he told me to load the rifle, I knew he was intent on carrying it out. The rifle was his "go to" weapon. He kept a pistol (that misfired half the time) in his bedroom drawer, but for road trips he always brought the rifle, and for our trips to Mexico he brought both.

Sometimes he pulled out the rifle for show. Clay got a glimpse of it the night we went on our first date; I was twenty-two and earning my own keep by then, but Dad still thought of me as his little girl, so when I didn't come home at the expected time he decided to try to find me. When Clay brought me home, Dad was waiting at the front door with a city map taped to the wall, scrutinizing it to figure out where Clay lived so he could track us down. Dad had the rifle within sight. I still don't know if he just staged all this while waiting for our arrival, or if he really intended to scour the entire city of Memphis looking for me. Whatever the case, he made a big deal out of me coming home an hour later than expected. I'm still surprised Clay asked me out for a second date. Perhaps he thought he'd better.

The rifle came in pretty handy on Vance Street as well. One night when I was about twelve, lying in my bed reading, I heard a knock on my bedroom window. My room was the closest to the street and adjacent to the front porch. At first I ignored the knock, thinking it was just the wind, but it got louder and more rapid. Then I figured it was the neighborhood boys playing a trick on me, so I waved and went back to my reading. But the knocking continued and I finally got up and went to the window. Peeking through the venetian blinds, I saw a man's hand holding a magazine; the man's body was hidden except for his hand and part of his arm. I froze. When I looked again, the man had opened the magazine and was showing me a picture of a nude body. While I stood there in a daze, he turned the page and showed me another nude. I turned around, walked slowly toward my bedroom door, and then ran down the hallway as fast as I could and found my dad in the kitchen.

When I told him what had happened, he grabbed the rifle and headed for the front porch. The man was gone, but my dad ran up the street with the rifle in his hands, looking for him. The police, making the rounds of the neighborhood in their cruiser, saw him carrying the weapon; naturally, they stopped and questioned him. After hearing his explanation, they assured him they understood. Apparently they had been called to the scene by several neighbors reporting a "Peeping Tom."

The officers told Dad to take his rifle home and keep me handy so I could identify the man who had scared me. Within ten minutes the police had caught the peeper, and Dad escorted me to the police car where I was asked to take a look at the man sitting in the back seat. All I could identify was the color of his hand and the type of coat sleeve I had seen through the blinds, but it was enough.

The police hauled off the perpetrator, and Dad put his rifle back in the closet.

I had seen Dad partner with the twenty-two on many occasions. It always concerned me when he pulled it from the closet—like the night he ran in from the backyard, grabbed the rifle, and ran back out again. I watched from the kitchen window as he pointed the gun at a man trapped by our tall wooden fence and trying desperately to escape. Dad had recognized the man from the news that night; his name was Putt, and he'd already killed several people in the area, most of them in older apartment buildings like ours with closed-in hallways that could hide a killer from passers-by. He was probably going to enter our building from the back and make our tenants his next victims, but changed his mind when my dad spotted him.

I know my dad was scared when he saw this serial killer, but his adrenalin was pumping, and he knew he had to do something. He always wanted to be a hero, and who knows, maybe he was that night. Even though Putt climbed the fence and got away, perhaps my dad saved one of our tenants, or maybe even one of us, from a horrible fate. Putt was eventually caught, but not before killing several other people. Looking back, I have to say I am proud of my dad for being willing to take on a maniac in order to protect his family and friends. He really was a hero…and no one knew it.

And now, as we traveled the dark, desolate Texas highway, he was my hero again. For all the times he made me feel vulnerable with his angry tirades and depression, there were just as many when he made me feel safe and secure—like now. Although I was a bit nervous about the two men following us, I had faith that my dad's plan would get us out of this scary situation. He knew that sooner or later we'd run out of gas, and he didn't want us to be sitting ducks. His plan was to slow down and let them catch up with us, then scare them off by shooting at them.

But before he could carry out his plan, something wonderful happened: just over the horizon there appeared a gas station, and just beyond it was an exit ramp that circled back to the other side of the interstate. Dad told me he was going to bet that the two men needed gas as badly as we did, and would stop to fill up their car. But because our truck had two gas tanks, he felt we could make it to the exit ramp, circle back behind them, head in the opposite direction, and get away. And that is exactly what happened. When the men pulled into the gas station, we sped up and made it to the exit ramp as fast as we could. We crossed over the interstate and re-entered the highway going the opposite way.

When we passed we could see them gassing up, and they never even looked our way, not realizing we had circled back. We waited on the other side of the interstate, watching them from a distance. They got back in their car and drove quickly away, as if trying to catch up with us, not knowing we had turned around. We waited about an hour, until my dad felt sure they were very far down the road, and then we drove to the nearest exit ramp and re-entered on the opposite side to continue our journey. We stopped at the same gas station and filled up both our tanks. Those two gas tanks, and my dad's level head, probably saved our lives. I put the rifle back under the seat and whispered a prayer of thanks.

MR. HYDE

To me there is a kind of irony in the fact that my dad could be so calm and level-headed one minute, and so irrational the next. There were times I could talk to him about anything, and he was full of wisdom and understanding. These were the moments I cherished. There were other times when he betrayed my confidence. When I was in high school I had two very good guy friends: one I loved, and the other loved me. We spent a lot of time together, sometimes at my house. I had asked my dad not to embarrass me by addressing me in a negative way in front of these two friends, and he had assured me he would not. That was during one of his normal weeks.

One evening these two guy friends appeared at my door. I was hesitant to invite them inside as my dad had been having an episode that day. I could only hope he would remember his promise to me. As it turned out, he did exactly the opposite of what I had asked.

We had argued earlier about something trivial, but he was still angry with me and decided to use my friends as a means to discipline me. He said in front of them that he knew I didn't want him to embarrass me, so I needed to listen to him and do what he said without question. He then continued by addressing my friends directly and sharing with them the details of our "for family only" spat, emphasizing my rebellious attitude. They grew red faced, embarrassed for me and angry at my dad for using this tactic. After my dad left the room I teared up. In order to spare me further hurt, my friends pretended not to notice and excused themselves. I don't remember them ever returning to my house. I never confided in my dad again.

One minute I felt like I had the greatest dad in the world; the next minute I wished he were somebody else's dad. It was like living with Dr. Jekyll and Mr. Hyde. Ironically, this was one of my dad's favorite movies, yet he never recognized himself in the character played so convincingly by his screen idol, Spencer Tracy. Dad was Mr. Hyde the night he kicked in the television, the afternoon he smashed a china plate by throwing it against the wall, and the day he violently swiped all the writing tablets from the table where he was working.

I remember these things happening when I was a young girl and my grandmother was still alive. Although my dad loved his mother dearly, she seemed to bring out the beast in him just as Ingrid Bergman's character did to Spencer Tracy's in the movie. That was another irony: that he fought the hardest with the one he loved the most. And just like Mr. Hyde, he would run back to his bedroom and sleep it off, awaking as the good and decent Dr. Jekyll once again.

He could be well-mannered when he wanted to be, up to a point. A few years ago when my two sons brought their fiancées home to meet us, I put together a dinner for the entire family. Dad was the perfect Dr. Jekyll, and the girls loved him. While we were all playing a game in the living room, my brother Steve recalled an incident from our childhood when Dad had kicked over the breakfast Steve had made for him. Neither Steve nor I could remember what had made Dad mad that time, and if Dad could remember he wasn't saying. He just sat there smirking through the whole story, and of course we all laughed, including the boys' future wives; but in truth it was not a very funny memory.

We had been camping somewhere out west, on a three-month road trip we had taken to California, and were parked at a campsite. Something Steve said made Dad very angry, and after a bitter verbal exchange, Dad stormed off. After he left, Steve felt bad about the argument and thought he would do something nice for Dad by making him breakfast. Steve was only about fourteen at the time, and his culinary skills were nothing to brag about, but he cracked half a dozen eggs and scrambled them up in a skillet over the open campfire beside our trailer.

Dad returned and asked my brother what he was doing, and Steve told him he was sorry they had argued, and that he had made breakfast for him. My dad walked over to the campfire and kicked the frying pan, sending the eggs all over the ground. I will never forget the look on my brother's face. I felt so sorry for him; I wanted to cry, but I was too shocked to cry. I could only stare in disbelief at what my dad had just done. Mr. Hyde had resurfaced, and there was nothing we could do about it.

The very fact that Steve retold this story year after year at our family gatherings is a good indication that the scrambled egg incident affected him deeply, just as many of the things I retold year after year affected me. The story Steve told reminded us of several others, and we continued to bombard our company with ghosts from the past. By the end of the evening Elliot's fiancée was in tears—and not from laughing. Her sensitive nature reminded us just how dysfunctional our family really was. Retelling the stories as adults and laughing about them was our way of dealing with the pain.

You think things like that don't affect you, but they do. You think that as time goes by you get over it, and you forget about it, but you don't. It is true that you forgive. And it is true that there are many wonderful things that push the bad memories aside. But they do not blot out the bad memories; they only make them bearable. When you love someone, as we loved our father, you don't want to dwell on the bad; but since you cannot erase the bad from your memory, you learn to turn it into funny stories that you retell over and over when all the family gets together. The only problem with this is that although it is a type of healing for the wounded, it is a reminder to the one who did the wounding that his actions were tragic.

Such was the case with our family. Once we grew up and married and had families of our own, we would recount to our children many of the stories of our childhood. Those stories included, of course, some of the more memorable events of our life with Les. We laughed at all the antics, the unfinished projects, and the bouts of anger indulged in by our dad over the past fifty years. We did this in his presence, not really considering the hurt and guilt this heaped upon him. He always acted as if it didn't bother him, but I'm sure it did. It was not our intent to hurt him; it was the only way we knew of dealing with the pain of living with a bipolar dad.

Perhaps if our dad had changed, we could have put the past behind us once and for all, and not brought it up again even in fun. But the sad truth is that he never changed. He did get a little more mellow with age, or maybe he just got a little more tired, and didn't have the strength to put up the same kind of fight. But he never outgrew his bipolar condition, and endured its cyclical episodes until the end of his days.

A perfect example of this was during the last week of his life when we took him to the hospital. The nurses experienced first-hand what it was like to live with Dr. Jekyll and Mr. Hyde.

"We just love Mr. Ash," smiled the adorable young nurse who popped into the room when I returned from lunch. "He is the cutest thing," she continued, tucking his sheets around him. "I just want to take him home with me. All the nurses do. He is so sweet."

Mom and I just looked at each other, wondering how long it would take before they discovered Mr. Hyde. It only took one day. That night we got a phone call at three o'clock in the morning. I was upstairs sleeping in my mom's bed, and she was sleeping where she had camped out for the past nine months, on the couch next to my dad's easy chair. The couch had become her bed because she couldn't be more than ten feet away without him calling her name relentlessly. I heard the phone ring, and my mom scrambling to find it next to her pillow.

"Hello...Les, is that you?" she asked, half asleep. "Audrey is upstairs in bed...I said, she is asleep, and so was I. It's three o'clock in the morning!..(pause) Go back to bed, Les. (pause) Oh, all right!...Audrey!"

I wanted to ignore it. I was totally tapped out from the day's ordeal. We had taken Dad to the doctor, and after his examination we were told he had to be admitted to the hospital immediately. His diabetic legs were raw from lack of circulation, and pus was oozing from the sores on his feet. Mom had tried to take care of him as best she could, but he needed professional nursing care, and the doctor knew that the best thing for him (and my mom) was a few days in the hospital. We had started our day at six that morning and hadn't come home from the hospital till close to ten at night. My brother, my mom, and I all fell into bed as soon as we got home, savoring the prospect of an undisturbed night's sleep.

"Okay, I'm coming!" I yelled as I threw my covers aside. I stumbled down the stairs and took the phone.

"What's going on, Dad?" I asked, as if I didn't understand why he was calling.

But I did understand. He hadn't been away from my mom for more than a couple of hours in a very long time.

And he had certainly not been all night without her. I tried to explain that the doctor had ordered rest for Mom, and that we'd be back first thing in the morning. But the more I tried to explain, the louder and angrier he became. I could hear the nurse in the background trying to calm him down.

"You come up here right now and take me home!" he yelled into the phone.

"I can't come up there right now, Dad," I told him calmly. "We're all in bed, and you need to go back to bed too. If you will just go to sleep, we'll be there when you wake up." I thought I could reason with him; I should have known better.

"You come up here right now!" he ordered again.

"I can't do that, Dad," I repeated.

"Are you refusing to do what I'm telling you to do? I'm your father, and I'm telling you to get up here right now!"

"Dad, I am not going to come up there."

"The hell you're not!"

"Please, Dad," I pleaded, "go back to bed."

But it didn't do any good. He just got louder and more out of control, and I knew I could not reason with him. I made one final attempt to calm him down before I told him I was hanging up the phone.

"Dad, I know you're upset, but we will be there first thing in the morning. I am very tired, and I'm going to have to hang up and go back to bed."

"You're hanging up on me?" he screamed in Robert De Niro fashion. "You're hanging up on me, your father? You are hanging up on me? Who told you you could hang up on me?"

I knew better than to say "God." He would use that one against me, and tell me that God had told him I should obey him. I said the only thing I could say to answer his question.

"I did."

I closed the cell phone and went back to bed. As I lay there I thought about how strong I had become. There was a time when I would have been unable to hang up on my dad, when it wouldn't have mattered that I was bordering on delirium due to exhaustion; I would have thrown on some clothes as quickly as possible and driven the forty-five minutes to the hospital to appease him. It was how he had raised me. The father is the boss; you do exactly what the father says without hesitation or question. So also with teachers, preachers, police, doctors, government officials: all were to be obeyed without question—a strange indoctrination coming from a man who questioned everything. It shaped the way I perceived myself, as submissive and obedient, and had enabled male adults to take advantage of me at an early age and get away with it. But I was stronger now, and had learned to say No.

The next morning when we arrived at the hospital, the cute little nurse that had burbled with pleasure over my dad was not so bubbly anymore. It seems my dad had caused quite a ruckus, and it had taken half the staff to calm him down after I hung up. It took several nurses and a heavy dose of medication to get him to stop yelling and disturbing all the other patients. But to look at my dad the next morning, you would never know it. Mr. Hyde had been drugged and forced to sleep, but it was Dr. Jekyll who woke up the next morning. He was as sweet as he could be. A new nurse arrived on the scene with the shift change…and she wanted to take my dad home.

THE TENANTS

No one was more exposed to the faces of Dr. Jekyll and Mr. Hyde than our tenants. The apartments were four to a building, with two downstairs and two upstairs; there were two such buildings, divided by a driveway, making a total of eight apartments. There was no central heat or air conditioning, so in the summer we kept our windows open, and everybody knew pretty much everybody else's business. If my dad was mad, everyone knew it. If he was involved in a new invention, every tenant knew the details. And if he was happy, they could hear him singing and dancing to his favorite big bands. Nothing was hidden, and nothing was sacred at 1191 and 1199 Vance Street.

Because our tenants stayed with us for long periods, some as long as twenty years, they were more like family than tenants. My grandmother Bernice was the original landlady and kept the property in mint condition. If there was a problem of any kind, plumbing or electrical, she fixed it immediately. If an apartment needed painting, she would stay up all night and have it completely finished by the time the rest of us woke up. She kept the grounds in immaculate shape, with rose gardens and neatly edged walkways, as well as a beautiful vegetable garden in the backyard.

As long as my grandmother was living and healthy, our apartments were a showcase of beautifully crafted workmanship. Each one boasted hardwood floors and ten-foot ceilings. Some had fireplaces, while others had intercom systems. A few even had dumbwaiters, the old-fashioned type with pulleys and bells. In their day, the apartment buildings were home to the classiest of residents.

Such was our upstairs tenant, Mrs. Reeves, who was quite the spinster and matriarch of the building. She was one of the original tenants, already living there when my grandmother purchased the property. My grandmother had saved quite a bit of money from the boarding house she had owned on Monroe Street next to her sister, Nell. Bernice and Nell were very close, and both were very good businesswomen, taking old homes and turning them into multiple dwellings for families with soldiers coming home from the war. The returning soldiers flocked to my grandmother's house, where she provided meals and a place to stay. There was a small apartment for my mom and dad, who had also returned from the service.

With the profits she had saved from this boarding house, my grandmother eventually had enough to purchase the two very lovely apartment buildings on Vance Street, just a few blocks from where her sister lived. My dad had failed to persuade my grandmother to go further east; he believed Memphis was moving in that direction, and time proved him right, but my grandmother was loath to move too far away from her best friend and sister, Nell.

The two of them were inseparable. They had helped raise each other, their mother having died when they were very young. They went to the same church, next door to Aunt Nell's house. They shopped at the same grocery, grew the same roses and vegetables in their gardens, and enjoyed the same soap operas. They called each other every Saturday to watch wrestling on television, cheering for the same fake fighters. I think they liked the fights so much because they were both fighters themselves when it came to the challenges of life.

My grandmother was from a large farm family and had a strong will, with brains to match. Her favorite saying was "Where there's a will, there's a way!" Although her education was limited, she was wise and cunning and didn't mind hard work. She also didn't mind making her grandkids work. The difference between her and my dad was that Grandma would work alongside us, while Dad would simply assign the chores and show up when they were finished. Steve's job was to mow the grass; I had to clean the bathroom, as well as sweep the halls of both apartment buildings every Saturday. It was important to my grandmother that the apartments stay clean and beautiful. She took pride in them—for herself, and for her tenants.

Mrs. Reeves, the oldest tenant in our building, lived directly above us. I liked most of our tenants, but wasn't particularly fond of her. Mrs. Reeves was used to having everything a certain way and was impossible to satisfy. In the winter the apartment was too cold, in the summer too hot. The mail did not come on time. She needed new light bulbs. Our dog was barking too much. The faucet was dripping.

But the major complaint came every thirty days when we had to collect the rent: the seventy-five dollars she paid each month for her six-room apartment was too high. This was unreasonable of her, as most places charged far more. After several years of using good business practices my Grandmother finally paid off the mortgage and managed to raise the rent to a hundred dollars a month. But it's never easy to ask family for money, and although not blood kin, our tenants were closer to us than our own relatives.

I was about two when our family moved to Vance Street, and by the time I was ten I was the official rent collector for all the older tenants. I always dreaded climbing the stairs to collect from Mrs. Reeves. She invariably invited me in, because she was lonely and liked to chat a bit. She usually complained about my dad, who was slow in fixing her dripping faucet or attending to some other minor issue, and I would just nod and smile as I wiped the cobwebs from the sheet-covered chair where I sat. Her apartment was dark and smelled of musty perfume.

She tried to be nice by offering me candy, but it was always the hard kind that I didn't like; being polite I took it but never ate it. I would sit and listen to her talk of the old days when the apartments were among the more elite midtown dwellings. As one of the original tenants, she had the apartment with the dumbwaiter and intercom. She would tell me about the servants she used to have, and I imagined that in her day she ruled with an iron hand in a classy kind of way. I got the impression she had been a very successful career woman of some sort, probably in retail, as she alluded to fashion quite a bit. But times had changed, and she was old and hunched over and not so pretty anymore, and her dark clothes matched the surroundings of her room.

When she finally wound down for a few seconds, I would take advantage of the lull in the conversation to let her know that I had to get back downstairs where dinner was waiting for me. She would then go to her dresser, pull out an envelope with the seventy-five dollars, and place it in my hand as if it were her last. Just before closing her door behind me, she would remind me once more to tell my dad he needed to fix her dripping faucet. I assured her, as always, that he would get to it as soon as possible knowing he would not.

By the time Mrs. Reeves passed away, my grandmother was ill and my dad had become the new landlord. He rented Mrs. Reeves' apartment to a nice young man named Michael, who, surprisingly, was happy to take the dark musty apartment just the way it was; he said he would fix it up if my dad would deduct the expenses from the rent, and my dad agreed, glad to be relieved of the task of preparing the apartment for a new tenant. Michael soon began sub-renting to one of his friends without our consent, but we didn't object; the apartment was big and we knew Michael was a struggling young musician. But then his roommate brought in another young man, and before long there were more men living upstairs than we could keep track. Their apartment was right above us, and their bedroom right above mine.

I could hear them at night fighting like cats and throwing things. Sometimes I heard other noises that I dare not describe in this book. It turned out they were all lovers with a multitude of partners that changed every other week or so. Michael and his original roommate, Kevin, were the steady ones who lived there permanently, but the other men came and went. It was my first up-close experience with the gay lifestyle, and was eye-opening and interesting all at the same time.

The young men were pleasant and paid their rent on time. They also fixed up the dingy old apartment to be the most exquisite dwelling in our building; it could have been showcased on the Home and Garden channel! Needless to say, the older tenants were shocked when they discovered these young men were gay, but by this time things were changing in the midtown area of Memphis, and most people were getting used to the changes.

My dad was always kind and helpful to the young men, although he would be the first to tell you he disapproved of their lifestyle choice. Dad was a WWII veteran and the gay culture was particularly disconcerting to this older generation, but you would not find anyone more courteous to Michael and his friends than my dad. As for me, I was too young to even understand it. All I knew was that Michael needed a ride to work every day to play the piano, and on many an occasion I was his chauffeur.

Another tenant I was forced to visit every month was Mrs. Raines, a widow who lived across the driveway at

1199. She was a pleasant older lady whose constant companion was a parakeet she had taught to converse with her. She rarely complained except to ask for more heat in the winter, fixed whatever she could in her apartment by herself, and only asked for my dad's services when she could not take care of it personally, knowing full well that it would be weeks before he got around to it.

Once my dad started on a project, however, he put his whole mind, body, and soul into the task at hand. The only problem was that every project took three times longer than necessary—a perfect example being the time we had a sewer issue at 1199, the apartment building where Mrs. Raines resided. She had complained of a plugged toilet, to which my dad responded a little more quickly because the complaints were—as one would expect—relentless. Unable to get to the bottom of the problem from above, he decided to tackle it from below by digging a ten-foot trench all along our driveway, where the sewer pipes were located, to try and find the blockage. My brother was conscripted to help dig, while I was called upon to supply plenty of ice-cold sweet tea and lemonade.

Once Dad located the blocked pipe, he sawed it in two so he could get a look inside. He had asked the tenants not to flush their toilets while he was working on the sewer line, but because the project took such a long time, the tenants either forgot or became impatient. They invariably managed to flush just when my dad was looking straight into the pipe, sending a deluge of urine and feces straight into his face. I remember him yelling all kinds of profanities every time this happened, and I can't say I blamed him; it was a reeking mess. My dad took several weeks to finally fix the problem, after which he was too exhausted to fill in the trench, so my brother and I came to the rescue and finished the job.

Dad never held the toilet-flushing against Mrs. Raines; he was actually very forgiving about it all. In a way, the tenants were like our extended family. If one of them was struggling financially, he would not collect their rent that month. He would make sure the kids in the apartment building had toys at Christmas, and would spend his own money to ensure that none of them went without presents. If any of the tenants were going to be by themselves at Thanksgiving or Christmas, they would get an invite to our home for the holiday meal. And he always turned the old furnace up a notch around Christmastime.

The heat in our apartments was not regulated by the occupants of individual units; just like Fred Mertz, the landlord in "I Love Lucy," my dad had to go down to the basement to turn up the heat in the large steam furnace that fed the radiators in all the apartments. It was difficult regulating heat for eight different apartments with eight different ideas of just how much heat was necessary to stay comfortable. Needless to say, wintertime was when we received the most phone calls, and when I received the most complaints during collection of the rent money.

Heat was not a problem for the Bragg's, however. You couldn't find nicer folks than Mr. and Mrs. Bragg, the tenants who lived next door to Mrs. Raines. Never complaining or bothering anyone, and always paying their rent on time, they were probably the best tenants we had. They were a sweet elderly couple who had lived at 1199 since before our arrival. They loved my grandmother, and even my dad. I remember them for many things, but especially for the car my dad bought from them.

It was the first car I drove all by myself when I turned sixteen, and I thought it was beautiful. It was an antiquated black Ford sedan with wingtips and no power steering or power brakes, but I thought it was amazing. Mrs. Bragg sold it to us because Mr. Bragg had had surgery on his back and could no longer drive safely; they didn't want to take a chance on him getting out and getting hurt.

As it happened, it wasn't the getting out that killed him, but the staying in. He'd had a type of surgery that fused vertebrae together, making his back extremely straight and giving him little flexibility. As time went on and Mr. Bragg felt better, he did what he loved to do, which was sit on the porch—an evening ritual for the couple, as well as most of the other tenants in our buildings. All the apartments had porches big enough to hold several chairs and a table, which was perfect for relaxing on a warm summer night and watching neighbors stroll up and down the street.

I was sitting on our porch one late afternoon when I heard an awful scream coming across the driveway from the upstairs porch where Mr. and Mrs. Bragg were sitting—only no one was sitting. Mrs. Bragg was leaning over the rail with her hands on her face, screaming, looking down at the ground. I looked down to see what she was staring at, and there was poor Mr. Bragg lying stiff and straight, face down in the grass below. My dad, who had also heard the scream and came out to see what had happened, ran over to help Mr. Bragg, but there wasn't much he could do. Someone must have called for an ambulance, because within a few minutes one arrived. The hospital was just a couple of blocks away, and it didn't take long to get there, but Mr. Bragg died in the ambulance on the way.

According to his wife, Mr. Bragg had become restless and wanted to walk a bit on the porch. Intending to take a look at the roses below, he had leaned over the rail and lost his balance. But because of the fused vertebrae, he couldn't straighten back up when he started falling forward, and toppled over the rail. It was both sad and bizarre. Mrs. Bragg did not live in our apartments much longer after that. I never knew where she moved, but I'm sure she didn't want to be reminded of her husband's demise every time she sat on the porch. As for me, I thought twice about getting too close to the edge of anything not on ground level.

To this day, I steer clear of all balcony rails and half walls from second story up. I still picture poor Mr. Bragg falling head first onto the ground below.

Ceily was probably the craziest tenant that ever lived in our apartments. I had met her at church and befriended her. When I found out she had no where to live, I felt sorry for her and invited her to come to our place for a while. My dad allowed her to live in our apartments for a fraction of the rent. But it turned out Ceily had some real problems, and my parents never let me forget that I was the one who had brought her into our lives.

She had been in a car wreck several years earlier. The accident had left her mentally and emotional unstable, and she had to take medicine to keep some semblance of sanity for the sake of herself and those around her. She had a huge crush on the minister of our church, and would get up in the middle of his sermon and walk zombielike toward him with her hands raised. She would stand directly in front of him until the deacons came and physically carried her out of the sanctuary. She did this so many times, she finally had to be banned from entering the worship center.

Her apartment was right across the driveway from ours, and from my bedroom window I could look straight into her living room. She had no curtains and kept her blinds raised, so there was nothing hidden from anyone who glanced her way. On many occasions I saw her standing in front of the window as naked as a jay bird, with hands held high, staring and speaking to a picture of our pastor she had taped to her wall.

On other occasions she would walk out of her apartment naked and head down our street. My dad, who was the only one home, would have to go get her, take her back upstairs, and talk to her firmly as a father to a child. My dad was at his best when someone needed his help—and at his worst when he needed ours. Perhaps my dad understood Ceily so well because in some ways he was like her: they both had good days when they behaved perfectly normally, and other times when they acted like children.

Ceily was definitely the more childlike of the two; Dad only behaved like a child when his bipolar condition got the best of him, whereas Ceily behaved like a child whenever she came off her medicine, which was more often than not. She was a little lost orphan, and we all felt sorry for her. Eventually, we had to call someone to come and get her, since she was more than we could handle, and we couldn't afford to lose our other renters on account of her; the apartments were our livelihood. But we kept in contact with Ceily for many years, as we did with many former tenants who remained part of our lives even after they left Vance Street.

Dad was especially sad to see Ceily go. He had formed a bond with her that had connected them in a type of father and child relationship. He understood her, because like her, he had experienced cycles of pain in his own life. Dad never looked past a person or their problems. He always tried to put himself in their place; feel what they felt, think like they thought, see what they saw.

I can honestly say that my dad was one of the most fair-spirited men I ever knew. His "go to" saying was "Don't judge a man until you've walked a mile in his shoes." The lessons he taught me about how to see my fellow man stuck with me into adulthood—which is, I suppose, the reason I forgave him so easily when he wounded us: I tried to put myself in his shoes, and understand the torment he felt as a person with a mental condition. We always gave him a pass. He taught us to root for the underdog, and in my mind there was no greater underdog than my dad.

THE COMPASSION

I know that any compassion I have, I got from him. Never an ambulance went by that he didn't remove his hat and pray. Never did a funeral procession approach us that he didn't pull over, get out of the car, and place his hat over his heart. At every baseball game or tennis match we attended, he rooted for the losing team or player.

He also brought home every stray dog that crossed his path. At one point we had so many dogs, we had nowhere to put them; I came home from college one summer and thought our house had been rented to the RSPCA. There was Hobo, the homeless dog that followed me home from elementary school one afternoon, and Iggy, the dog someone left at our front door. Iggy was a beautiful white fluffy mix of something big; he was also very stupid and would run full tilt into walls. Maybe he was partially blind, but the name Iggy, short for "ignorant", seemed to fit.

Then there was Munchkin, my brother's brown dachshund, inherited by my mom and dad after the dog was run over and lost a leg. Big Red was big and red (go figure), and had been picked up on the interstate by my dad. Skuffy, also a stray, looked just like Dorothy's Toto on Wizard of Oz. Last but not least was Corrie Ten Boom, the pretty little cocker spaniel, named after the great World War II heroine who hid terrorized Jews from the Nazis. I taught Corrie how to fold her paws in prayer, which came in pretty handy in this house full of male mutts.

The problem of too many dogs was solved one afternoon when Skuffy and Big Red got into a skirmish over Corrie. Hobo and Iggy, too old to care much about such things, kept to themselves, but Big Red and Skuffy had been jockeying for Corrie Ten Boom's attention ever since they had arrived on the scene. At first it was quite innocent, but as the weeks rolled by, the two of them became more jealous of time spent with Corrie. Skuffy was usually the one who started the fights, thinking he was much bigger than he really was. If he could have just looked in a mirror, he might have had second thoughts about taking on Big Red, but as it turned out the fight cost him his life. One yank of Skuffy's scrawny little neck by Big Red, and it was over.

We were very sad. We didn't want to keep Big Red after that, but also did not want to have him put to sleep, as it wasn't really his fault. So we sent him where all convicted murderers end up: jail, almost literally. We found a home for him at a park that had once been a penal farm, where convicts worked off their sentences; one of the employees who worked and lived there took him, and Big Red spent the rest of his days in quiet non-violence.

Hobo and Iggy died shortly thereafter from old age, leaving only Corrie and Munchkin, who got along quite well. However, their friendship ended the day Munchkin committed suicide. He did not leave a note, but we believe he suffered from depression after the disappearance of the other dogs in the house. He was known for curling up under blankets to get warm, and on one particularly cold night he twisted himself up in the blanket again and again to the point where the threads wrapped around his neck and he strangled himself.

Our experience with dogs was as theatrical as our life with Les—sometimes amazing or comical, sometimes sad. I bet there aren't many dog lovers who've had in their midst a love triangle, a fight, a homicide, and a suicide. Truly, the makings of a movie for Animal Planet!

But while stray dogs were important to my dad, stray people were even more so. No person in need ever crossed our path without Dad stopping to help, and hitch hikers were the créme de la créme of stranded people in need. There were many times I had to move to the back seat so a strange man could take my place up front. Dad would tell me to sit directly in back of the hitchhiker, and be ready with the heavy flashlight he kept under the seat in case the man tried anything. I often asked my dad why he took so many chances and picked up strangers, to which he replied, "When I was in the service, we didn't have cars, and when we went on leave we depended on the charity of others to get us home."

The good news was, that by the time we came along, Dad was much more selective and cautious in choosing who to pick up and who to let be; and he never picked up someone if Mom was in the car; it made her terribly nervous…and Mom had good reason to be nervous. Dad hadn't always been so considerate of Mom's feelings on the matter. There was a day, regardless of Mom's objections, when he picked up every person he came across, including a man by the name of Norman Eugene Carter. If the name doesn't sound familiar, it's probably because you didn't live in Memphis in the early 50's. Norman Eugene Carter was an escaped convict, and on the FBI's most wanted list.

It was the month of December, and Dad decided to give himself an early present. He bought a black Oldsmobile Coupe with white leather seats. I have no idea how he could have afforded such a dream machine, but it was brand spanking new and it was his. One evening he wanted to show it off to some mutual friends, and invited the couple out for dinner and dance. The road to the club was on a pretty lonely stretch, and it wasn't long before my dad spotted a cab driver on the side of the pavement. The cabbie hailed them down and asked for a lift stating his taxi had run out of gas a few miles back. The man was in uniform, clean cut, nice looking, and had a winsome smile. Mom and Dad's friends were in the backseat, so dad motioned for Mom to scoot close to him, which allowed the man to sit in the passenger side with Mom squeezed between the two. Everyone exchanged names and the man introduced himself as Norman Carter.

Dad, being the friendly type, struck up a conversation with Norman, who was quite glib in his own right. The dialogue between the two men was both intelligent and friendly, until my dad began asking a few pointed questions about his taxi. Dad made the comment that he hadn't seen his stranded cab, to which Norman replied rather quickly that it was parked on a side road. Mom, sitting shoulder to shoulder with the man, felt in her gut that something was amiss, and asked if he had any identification. Norman smiled politely and said, "Sure." He reached inside his uniform coat, pulled out a gun, and aimed it right across my mom's face directly toward the side of my Dad's temple.

Norman Eugene Carter kidnapped my parents and their friends at gunpoint, forced them to drive down a side road, told them to get out of the car, and then helped himself to my dad's brand-spanking new convertible. Ironically, the two friends in the back had taken all their jewelry and stuffed it beneath the seat as soon as Norman pulled out his gun. Little did they know the escaped convict was going to steal the car. The two devastated couples walked for a mile before they found a gas station and a telephone. They called for help and waited. In the meantime, the police found the taxi on the side road, and a naked cab driver tied up inside.

Eventually, the police caught up with Norman, and there was a big shoot out. No one was killed, but Dad's car was strafed with bullets from side to side. It was drivable, but the car looked like a metallic piece of Swiss cheese. Dad had no insurance. The police, however, did have some good news to share - they had recovered the jewelry; that did not console my dad.

A year later my mom and dad were sitting at the dining table enjoying a bit of dinner while they watched the six o'clock news. Dad, being the sentimentalist that he was, suggested to Mom that they make a visit to the prison where Norman was incarcerated. He had been such a nice thief; he hadn't hurt anyone, not the cab driver, not the policemen, not them. They even talked about taking him a present; after all, it was Christmas, "peace on earth, goodwill toward men." Dad had no sooner gotten the words out of his mouth, when the newscaster announced the prison escape of Norman Eugene Carter. Without saying a word, my dad got up and locked the doors, while my mom closed all the curtains. They turned off the television, turned out the lights, and went to bed…but I doubt they got any sleep.

FAVORITE CHRISTMAS

Yes, Dad was a sucker for the stranded hitch hiker, the homeless hobo, and the wino lying in the gutter; he was especially sentimental and benevolent at Christmas. If one of the tenants was struggling financially, he would not collect their rent that month. He would make sure the kids in the apartment building had toys at Christmas, and would spend his own money to ensure that none of them went without presents. He made certain the widows in our apartments did not spend the holiday alone, and started a tradition of visiting the older tenants with Christmas goodies and a carol or two, a tradition I continued well into my teens.

When Dad passed me the "caroling baton" I solicited the help of my friend, Jeannie. I'd known Jeannie since third grade, and she was my best friend all through elementary school. When her mom was considering moving, I talked them into taking the vacant apartment next to ours at 1191. Even though the apartment was much smaller than the large house they had been leasing, they couldn't turn down the cheap rent. Jeannie and I were inseparable for many years until, sadly, we drifted apart in high school. But for a good portion of the time that she lived next door to me, we were like Lucy and Ethel on the "I Love Lucy" show. I usually came up with the crazy ideas, and she was my sidekick who helped me accomplish them.

Jeannie and I did everything together, which was an interesting phenomenon, because I was a tomboy and she was a very girly girl. In fact, I remember well that Jeannie had the cleanest socks in our class, a state of affairs pointed out by the teacher on several occasions. I was never one to stay indoors; as soon as I got home from school I found my favorite twins, the Chin boys from down the street, and we would play street ball or ride our bikes.

While I was outside getting my socks dirty, Jeannie was inside keeping hers clean.

Apart from Jeannie, my best friends were the neighborhood boys. Every summer we would stay out late and play all manner of games. Jeannie would participate from a distance, while I organized the activities. To keep my socks from getting too dirty I played barefoot, coming in every evening with black feet and smelling like a puppy dog. One of my favorite memories of Dad is how he often rubbed my legs at night to relieve muscle cramps.

As I got older the neighborhood boys became interested in a different kind of sport, and since I wasn't ready for that, we went our separate ways. I started going to a new church where there were lots of kids, and Jeannie came with me. We no longer hung out in the 'hood as much as we took part in the activities at church. There was lots to do there, and we developed new interests with new friends.

Later, as Jeannie and I grew up and grew apart, there were some traditions that held us together, such as the baking and delivering of Christmas cookies. Mrs. Raines was our favorite recipient, because she got such a kick out of it; I think it was the highlight of her Christmas. She would invite us in and have us sit near her piano while she played us her favorite Christmas carols. We would sing for her, and she would reward us with very rummy fruitcake. We pretended to eat it, spitting it into our napkins when she wasn't looking. After taking our leave of Mrs. Raines we'd make our way through the buildings, singing at the doors of all the other tenants before returning to my apartment for hot chocolate and marshmallows. Dad would then haul us around in the back of the old white cargo van, driving all over east Memphis to look for the most beautifully decorated Christmas yards.

One particular Christmas was more memorable than any other. My dad had started renovating the kitchen two years earlier. He had torn out the wallboard, leaving the studs exposed as well as the large pantry full of kitchen gadgets and food items. Needless to say, it looked hideous. My mother had been begging him for over a year to finish the project, but my dad, who moved at his own pace, let her pleas go in one ear and out the other.

The door frame leading into our kitchen was of a typical straight, ninety-degree-angle construction; Dad decided to take it down and turn it into an arched doorway. But because of the tedious process he employed, it took three months to do what would have taken an ordinary carpenter one or two days. After cutting a piece of plywood to size, he would gradually form it into an arc by soaking it in water for fifteen minutes every day and then bending it, making it a little rounder each time. This was a slow and painful procedure for all of us to watch, but to my dad it was a science he had developed, and he was quite proud of it.

At the end of three months the kitchen doorway was an archway; but it led into an ugly kitchen, with electrical wiring falling down between studs adorned with broken wallboard and pieces of stapled insulation. My mother was both exhausted and embarrassed by the never-ending project, and it was an embarrassment to me as well. I decided it was time to take back our kitchen. I didn't have the knowledge or strength to replace the broken studs and wallboard, so I did the next best thing: I covered it up. I spent the money in my Christmas savings account (which I started every January) to buy cloth, out of which I made curtains to cover the entire wall that had been ripped apart. That took about half my money. With the other half I bought vinyl tiles to replace the ugly, worn tiles on the kitchen floor.

I hid the homemade curtains and tiles at Jeannie's apartment next door until Christmas Eve. That night, after everyone went to bed, Jeannie and I hung the curtains and laid the new floor. Starting at midnight, we worked right through till six the next morning, as quiet as church mice while my parents slept. We were so tired we became giddy, and by the time we made it to the very last tile, we were too exhausted to glue it down. We sat on the spot where the tile belonged and laughed at silly jokes for the next hour. Finally we forced ourselves to finish the job, until everything was beautiful for my mom's new Christmas kitchen.

I gave Jeannie a big hug and told her to go home and get some sleep before her mom woke up and discovered her gone. I was too excited to sleep, so I woke everyone up. When I escorted my mom into the kitchen, she stared in disbelief and awe, trying to contain her emotions and the tears welling in her eyes. For over two years she had lived in a construction site, and now she had her own personal kitchen makeover; an original DIY renovation long before HGTV was a household name. My dad was also very pleased, having tired of the project himself a year earlier. It was something my mom talked about for years, and as for me and Jeannie…well, we had a great memory only Lucy and Ethel could top. It is still one of my favorite Christmases of all time.

THE APARTMENTS

We had numerous tenants come and go over the course of the twenty-plus years we lived on Vance Street. When my grandmother passed away (during my junior year in high school), the apartment buildings were completely paid for and we were debt-free. There had been many fights over money between my grandmother and my dad during those years. Dad always wanted to borrow money on the apartments for his business ventures, and

Grandma always held her ground with a definite "no." After all, it was her hard work and scrimping and saving that had made it possible to buy the apartments. Besides, she knew my dad's record: so far, he had failed at every enterprise he had started. Some of the failures were beyond his control, but more often than not, they were a result of his not following through and sticking it out when the going got tough.

After my grandmother passed away and the apartment buildings became my dad's responsibility, he did exactly what Grandma had feared all those years. He borrowed money on the buildings and got us into huge debt. We now had two apartment buildings mortgaged to the hilt, and nothing to show for it except a truckload of Mexican pots we unloaded at our great-aunt's farm, much to her dismay. The Mexican pots, velvet pictures, and wrought-iron plant stands were about the only items left from the "Going out of Business Sale" we'd had when we closed the shop.

The gift shop had been one of those businesses that my dad's so called best friend, Tommy P., had persuaded him to purchase. It is remarkable how many "sure things" Tommy P. talked my dad into buying. It is also worth noting that every one of the businesses my dad invested in was one that Tommy originally owned but was ready to unload. There was the vinyl siding business, the used car lot, a multitude of pyramid schemes, and then the gift shop. The gift shop was what I remembered best, because not only did my brother and I travel to Mexico to help my dad buy the merchandise, we also ran the shop.

Had there been child labor laws back then, my dad would have had a lot of explaining to do; however, there was a lot of good learned from the work ethic my dad instilled in my brother and me. Not that we learned from his example, for he himself was not much of a worker. No, we learned because we were forced to do the work my dad did not want to do. Les loved starting the businesses and making the plans, especially on paper, and he loved going to market and buying the goods. What he did not like was the selling—which is where my brother and I came in. We were his little salesmen; we worked the shop. I don't remember my dad ever being at the shop except to unload more merchandise. I do remember my brother being there all the time. I was there during the summer and on weekends.

Needless to say, growing up with a bipolar dad was stressful, and had residual negative effects that cannot be overlooked. More about that later. But one immediate effect was the demise of the apartment buildings. The fact that my dad allowed them to fall into such disarray, and become so encumbered by debt, was an indicator of just how sick he was.

By this time, my brother had moved to California to escape the mayhem and try to make a name for himself in the music business. I was in college four hours away, but came home every summer to work and pay my way through school. While at home I always took on a project related to our apartments, which had now become eyesores. There was no option to raise the rent, as the outside of the buildings needed painting and the inside was deteriorating due to lack of regular maintenance. The wiring was old, the plumbing leaked, the yard was neglected, and behind the apartments were junk-filled storage areas for my dad's used appliances and many unfinished projects.

But the worst and most embarrassing thing about the apartments for me was the roaches. As long as Grandma had been alive, there was not a roach in sight. But now they were everywhere. It was horrible to walk into the kitchen at night, hear the little scratchy sounds of insects moving about, turn on the light, and watch them scatter all over the counter, sink, and stove to disappear into cracks and crevices. When I had my friends over it was even more embarrassing. I worked hard to make sure they didn't follow me into the kitchen.

I still remember one evening when my best friend from church, Sarah, came to spend the night. We were being silly, and finding a wig in my costume box she put it on her head. A roach crawled out from under the wig, scampered down her cheek and fell onto her lap; of course she screamed as she swiped the roach from her lap onto the floor where I stomped it repeatedly. She was shocked. I was mortified. My sweet friend was so gracious, however, that she never said a word to anyone at church nor did she ever repeat the matter; she knew how much it bothered me. She never made a big deal out of it, but it was a big deal to me. I was ashamed that I lived in a house in which you could not even invite friends over without worrying about cockroaches.

The apartment buildings were getting worse all the time, and my dad was getting less and less interested in doing anything about them. We had already lost a couple of tenants, and at least two apartments were vacant, reducing our already limited income. Dad's bipolar condition didn't help, either. The apartments were a burden to him; they were beneath him. When he was manic, he thought up ways to make big money, spending hours outlining grandiose schemes on paper until our dining room table was covered with sketches, newspaper clippings, and sheets of ideas. He would make his job the creation of beautiful dreams. Paper dreams.

One of his favorite pastimes was to go through old magazines and cut out pictures. He kept an alphabetized picture file of assorted colorful photographs. He also collected cards, quotes he liked, and short stories. All these he kept in his personal folders, most of which lay on the dining room table year in and year out. Our apartment had been immaculate as long as my grandmother was alive, but after her passing we could easily have been candidates for social services.

My mom, tired from work, never had the energy or personality to stand up to my dad. So even though she longed to have a pretty home, she just learned to live with the mess, as we all did. I lived in organized clutter for the latter part of my teenage years, a situation more embarrassing for me than for my brother, who had already moved out. My best friend from college, Joanna, still recalls how she came over to my house one day to discover our refrigerator lying in pieces all over our living room floor. She found the scene highly entertaining.

I never knew what project my dad would tackle next. He always had something torn apart and scattered all over the house, and since he never finished a project before he started another, our home was always a disorderly array of electrical and plumbing supplies and fixtures, wood and metal scraps, and other bits and pieces. It looked like a small appliance repair shop, warehouse, and hobby store all in one. Had reality shows been as popular as they are today, we would have been on every producer's list for "Hoarders," "Surreal," and "Intervention." Our family's collection of dysfunctions was so fascinating, I have no doubt the ratings would have soared, and we would have been seasonal favorites for years.

Joanna shared other memories of my dad at his funeral. She said she "loved Mr. Wilson because he had such a zest for life." I will say that about my dad. He really did have a zest for life. The manic side of him always brought great excitement and happiness—until the high played out, and he started coming down from the mountaintop into the pit of depression. Some of his plans for the apartments were actually quite beautiful on paper, but they required money, and money was something we did not have. And not having money sent him spiraling down, down, down.

The more he spiraled, the more the apartments spiraled downward with him. What had once been very profitable was now a liability. Because my dad was not a practical man, he had a hard time seeing to the things that would keep the tenants happy; the only reason most of them stayed was because the rent was so cheap. It was a catch twenty-two; the cheap rent kept them from moving, but it gave us no margin of profit to maintain the buildings properly or make a dent in our mortgage payments. I knew something had to be done soon, or we would lose the apartments to the bank, and all of us would end up on the street.

I convinced my dad we needed to sell the apartments. I had a friend whose father was in real estate, and we asked him to sell the apartments for us. In the meantime, I got busy painting the outside of the buildings to give them more curb appeal. Even though the apartments were brick, there was a lot of wood around the windows and door frames, as well as the huge columns that held up the outside porches on both stories. The paint on these was peeling and in desperate need of scraping and sanding before painting could even begin. It was a major undertaking, but we could not afford to hire a painter, so the job was left to me.

Earlier that summer my dad had brought home a homeless drug addict named Billy and given him the job of painting our apartments, but the man left such a mess that it only made the job more difficult, as he had painted more brick than wood. I spent half my time correcting his mistakes. Bringing home displaced men was nothing new for my dad; when he didn't bring them home, he took them to get a sandwich at a nearby fast food restaurant. Most of the time they wanted cash for hard liquor, but Dad only gave them money as a last resort. If they asked for work, Dad would find something for them to do at our apartments after instructing Mom to set another place at the table. Such was the case of Billy who came for dinner and never left.

Dad spent the next year and a half trying to get and keep Billy drug free. He made a room for him up in our floored attic. The attics of the apartment buildings were as large as two apartments put together; lots of headroom and very private. Dad did not discover until much later that not only had Billy never quit doing drugs, he kept a nice supply on hand under his cot in his attic apartment, which did not sit well with my dad. Drugs and alcohol were two vices my dad was definitely against. His own father had been a mean drunk, and his stepfather had been killed by someone under the influence. I heard the story at least once a year of how Granddad Shumaker had stopped by the side of the road to change a tire, and a doctor coming home from a party three sheets to the wind hit him head on, pinning him between both cars. He died instantly.

My mom's dad was a friendly drunk. He was part Irish and loved his whiskey. Every Friday evening after a week of working nine to five as a plumber, he would take a small detour to the neighborhood pub where he would spend a designated portion of his earnings on getting happily intoxicated. He would then walk the remainder of the way home, where my mom's mom would welcome him lovingly and help him into his favorite chair.

Like me, my mom had embarrassing issues with her dad. Unlike mine, they were not about work or temper tantrums, but about alcohol. Whenever my mom had boys over to court her on Friday nights, Granddad would unknowingly embarrass her by popping into the parlor and carrying on in a friendly fog of drunkenness. Grandmother, quite the pragmatic, soon found a solution to this distressing dilemma. She acquired some rope and instituted a Friday night ritual of tying my grandfather into his favorite chair in the basement, with the radio turned up to drown out his happy but off-key singing.

Needless to say, given this background on both sides of the family, the Les Wilson household regarded alcohol as a scourge. So when Dad saw a wino laying helpless in a gutter, he could not look the other way. It was the same when he met the drug addict, Billy, who was also in much need of help.

I don't know how Dad found Billy. Perhaps Billy found him; I think my dad must have had his name scribbled on the back of every bathroom stall in every liquor store in Memphis. All I know is that one day a wild-eyed, unshaven, unkempt young man came to dinner one night and never left. Billy lived in our attic for the first part of the summer, eventually making his way into one of our rental apartments, where he and Jeannie's sister fell in love. It was not the best situation; it seems Billy loved the bottle and the drugs more than he loved Jeannie's sister. They eventually realized their mistake and went their separate ways. Jeannie's sister met a wonderful man a couple of years later and lived a very fulfilled and happy life, while Billy continued to travel down the path of drugs and despair.

The apartment buildings, like Billy, also continued to travel down a path of despair. One day while up on a twenty-five-foot ladder, I heard a man calling to me from below. He was quite impressed with a nineteen-year-old girl who would dare to don a painter's cap and take on such a monumental task. We got into a conversation about the apartments, and he asked if I thought my dad would be interested in selling them to him. He wanted to fix them back up to their original state and sell them as condominiums. The man's name was Mr. Dupree.

He asked me to offer a thousand dollars to the other realtor to negate the contract Dad had just signed a couple of days earlier. The realtor accepted, leaving us free to sell the apartments to Mr. Dupree, which is exactly what we did. Mr. Dupree gave us three months to clear out all our belongings and vacate the premises before his bulldozers arrived to start tearing down the dilapidated carports in the back. This was a very reasonable amount of time to get everything in order for a move—if you were normal. But Dad was not normal, and he had his own way of handling preparations for moving.

Instead of clearing out the antiques in the two large attics and basements, he spent the first month of our three-month window washing out plastic plant cups he had stored in the garage after the gift shop had closed. These plastic plant cups were practically worthless, whereas the antiques in the attics were priceless; yet he thought that what he was doing was logical. So once again it was left up to me to contact dealers to come and make offers on the furniture and household goods from the attics and basements.

Then there was the problem of disposing of the used appliances stored in the garages and carports behind the buildings. Some were working and some were not, but who knew which was which. Two of our three months had now come and gone, and we still hadn't packed up our own apartment or had time to look for a new place to live. I decided to let the appliances go and start looking. My dad, on the other hand, did not see the importance of looking for another place to live. He seemed to be in a fog of denial about the move ever happening.

Concerned about the broken-down appliances in the back, Dad decided he wasn't going to let Mr. Dupree steal them from him. Not that Mr. Dupree wanted them; what he wanted was to get rid of them as junk. So, when Mr. Dupree brought in his bulldozer, Dad's temper flared, and he pulled out his rifle. We managed to convince him that we were not living in the Old West, and that the legal contracts he had signed prohibited him from engaging in this type of gunfight at the "not OK" Corral. My dad decided to take his fight to the bedroom, where he nursed his grievance in peace, and I talked Mr. Dupree into giving us a little more time.

My dad did virtually nothing to help with this major move, retreating instead into his own little world. Perhaps the work involved in selling and getting rid of what we couldn't take with us seemed insurmountable to him. I think there was more to it than that, though. We had lived on

Vance Street for the past twenty-plus years, and Steve and I had grown up there. Besides, our family consisted of more than just the five of us who lived in apartment number two; our family also consisted of the tenants occupying the other nine flats in our buildings. Dad dreaded losing them as family and friends. And last but not least, I think he felt a great sense of loss in leaving the home he had shared for so long with his mother. Grandma Bernice had been the *grande dame* of 1191 and 1199 Vance Street, and moving brought finality to the fact of her passing. The apartments were Grandma's crowning achievement; leaving them was like leaving her. Dad went into a kind of depression which made him useless, spending his time on meaningless tasks while I tackled the major undertakings involved in the move.

I was the one who brokered the deal and sold the apartments. I contacted the dealers to clear out our attics and furnished apartments. I searched for a place to live and found a fitting home for us, one that we could afford with what little money we had left after paying our second and third mortgages. I held the moving sales to get rid of all the furniture and belongings we didn't have room to take with us. And finally, I made the arrangements for the actual move from the apartments to our new house, located out east where my dad had wanted to live years earlier.

By this time I'd had my fill of the "Samford and Son" apartments and was ready to leave, yet it was a very hard move for me emotionally. There were so many memories attached to that place! After all, I had lived there for twenty-two years. All my childhood experiences had taken place at 1191 Vance Street—and there had been some very good experiences, ones that I would cherish.

One such extraordinary experience was our trip out west in the homemade trailer we built in our backyard the summer after third grade, when I was eight and my brother was fourteen.

THE TRIP OUT WEST

The trip out west had been a dream of my dad's for a long time, and he was determined to carry it out. This was going to be the mother of all trips—the vacation to make up for all the summers we'd gone without one. Clearly, a three-month road trip to California and back would require a recreational vehicle of some sort, so my dad looked into purchasing a used one, but they were all too expensive. He finally decided to build his own. I don't know where he got the money to buy the materials needed to build the trailer, or to buy the old blue station wagon to pull it, but somehow he managed, and the project began that spring.

All the tenants watched in amazement as we built a wooden crate above a six-by-ten-foot chassis. The original chassis was a six-by-six-foot utility frame my dad had purchased at Sears, designed for a small trailer. In typical Les Wilson fashion, he enlarged it by using an old iron bed frame that he cut to size and then bolted to the utility trailer frame with the help of my brother. It was an extremely tedious process, as my dad used only a hacksaw to cut the iron bed frame and hand tools to bolt the parts together. He and my brother then reinforced the frame with dozens of two-by-twos and plywood.

Dad threw himself full-bodied into this project, working day and night. It continues to amaze me that he could accomplish truly remarkable things when he set his mind to it. I wondered what distinguished this project from the many he had abandoned unfinished, and thought it was the fact that this was for a "fun" trip he'd envisioned for years.

I learned later that Dad thought he was dying. Steve told me that Dad had been passing blood in his colon and thought he had cancer. He did not go to the doctor, afraid to hear the bad news; but, convinced in his heart that he only had a few months left, he resolved to make this once-in-a-lifetime trip with his family. That was what kept him focused and energized until construction of the trailer was completed. He never let on, and I'm glad I didn't know; it would have spoiled the trip for me. I am sad that my dad went through that needless worry, but perhaps a keen awareness of mortality was the motivation he needed to see the trip through.

The construction took a couple of months. I remember my dad and brother doing most of the actual building of the trailer, but I hammered quite a few nails myself. I was also responsible for picking up all the trash and retrieving any broken nails, bolts, or screws that happened to fall into the gravel. I did make one important contribution to the trailer's design: the idea for a small awning to be built over the entrance to keep out the rain. It turned out to be a great success.

My brother thought of a way for us to sleep. He came up with the idea of a folding bed made of plywood, much like that found on a sleeper car in a passenger train. The bed folded down at night and was wide enough for both my brother and me to fit longways. In the daytime it could be folded back up and out of the way, leaving room for a sitting area beneath to be used when the trailer was not in motion. The sitting area was also where my dad slept at night.

Steve also designed a makeshift shower. He and my dad built a small closet with a hole in the roof above it. A large container of water could be poured down on the person below by using a funnel to channel the water through the hole in the roof. The funnel was attached to a flexible plastic hose with a sprayer, and there was a drain in the bottom of the closet for the water to exit to the ground beneath the trailer. We also had a portable toilet that fit in the closet in the event we needed privacy for these more personal activities. Most of the time we used the facilities provided at campsites, but every now and then when there was nothing close by, we used our makeshift shower and toilet. It was every Boy and Girl Scout's dream.

Along with the shower and toilet we had a sink, a propane stove, and an icebox—a literal one that had to be kept cool with blocks of ice. We also had a built-in table and bench positioned between the sleeping/sitting area and the kitchen/bathroom area. All in all, it was a pretty nifty trailer, one we were proud to show off. And show it off we did, much to the delight of tenants and neighbors. Everyone in the neighborhood was fascinated with the design and structure of the trailer. The fact that it was covered in corrugated aluminum only made it more intriguing, and anyone who saw it asked to have a look inside.

Finally the big day came for us to hitch up the hillbilly RV and start our journey. The tenants and neighbors sent us off with baked goods and sandwiches while making side bets that we wouldn't make it past the Memphis-Arkansas Bridge. But everyone was excited that we were finally on our way. I'm sure the tenants were relieved that the endless hammering had stopped and they could have a three-month reprieve from my dad and his projects. My grandmother was happy to get her yard back and to have some peace for a while. My mom was eager to get on the road, as her four weeks of vacation had dwindled to three due to delays in construction. My brother and I were just plain excited, and as far as my dad was concerned—well, let's just say he was in rare manic form.

I remember pulling into the Gulf station at the end of our street and filling up with gas. Glen, the owner, came out to help us, and summoned all his employees to come and take a look at the homemade trailer; he and his men also made bets that we wouldn't make it past the Memphis-Arkansas bridge. My dad just smiled as he showed off his pet project, as well as the miniature fans he had installed in the station wagon to keep us cool along the way (there was no air conditioning). Before we pulled away, my dad made a five-dollar side bet with Glen that we would make it all the way to California and back.

As the gas station shrank in the rearview mirror, we headed toward downtown and the bridge. My heart began to pound as we neared the bridge, and when we reached it my brother and I exchanged nods of anxious anticipation. My mom sat with eyes closed, exhausted from all the midnight packing and preparations for the trip. My dad started singing, "California, here we come." I looked out the window and watched the tugboats floating effortlessly beneath us as they pulled large cargo on the Mississippi River. Steve saw it, too, and I could tell by the look on his face that he was thinking the same thing I was: if we could just make it across this bridge, we would be home free.

I closed my eyes and held my breath, listening as the trailer bumped across the ridges on the bridge. When my brother let out his breath I knew we had reached the other side, and I opened my eyes. The two of us looked at each other and smiled with relief as we leaned our heads back against our seats. Then we both joined Dad in singing the rest of the song. We had crossed the bridge, and all bets were off.

I don't remember too much about the trip out, except that it took several days to reach California; we made few stops, as we were intent on getting to Hollywood, my dad's Mecca. He had always dreamed of living the silver screen life, and in many ways had lived it vicariously through the movie stars he so admired. I grew up watching all the old MGM and Warner Brother movies, along with the RKO black-and-white classics. Dad was also a big fan of the silent films; his stepdad had worked in a theater company in Baltimore and introduced Dad to several silent screen stars when he was a young boy.

When we pulled into Hollywood with our homemade aluminum trailer, we really did look like the Beverly Hillbillies. In fact, we got stopped by quite a few folks who wanted to know if we were doing a pilot for some new sitcom. Anxious to get to her parents' house, my mom took a bus to San Francisco, leaving the rest of us to fend for ourselves in Tinseltown. Dad was truly in his element. Even though everything we did was about fulfilling his fantasies, he made it enjoyable for us as well. The one thing more important to him than Hollywood was his family, and he made it a priority to show us a good time while simultaneously trying to get a glimpse of every star and starlet he could.

We visited the backlots of many of the studios. Although not as vibrant as they had been in the thirties and forties, they were still enchanting, with lots of sets and small town façades; my favorite was the Old West. The highlight of our visit to the studios was when we spotted Robert Goulet entering the gate in his red convertible; he actually spoke to my dad and told him he had a very pretty little girl. Dad enjoyed telling this story over and over, and I loved hearing it.

After visiting the studios we took a trip down to Grauman's Chinese Theater, where all the movie stars' handprints and names are cemented in the sidewalk. Dad pointed out every name and shared some small tidbit about each actor represented in concrete. We placed our feet in a hundred different stone prints and then made our way to the Brown Derby, famous for its star-studded clientele. Although we could not afford to eat at the restaurant, Dad talked the hostess into letting us take a peek inside.

We were mesmerized by all the black-and-white silhouettes of famous profiles covering the walls.

We then hung outside for a while, trying to catch a glimpse of any celebrity. Dad finally spied a "not so famous" actor, and instructed me to go and get an autograph; *he* wanted the autograph, but he wanted *me* to ask for it. I didn't want to, but I knew better than to argue with him, so I did as I was told, much to my own embarrassment.

Les was truly in Hollywood heaven. If there was ever anyone who lived life through movies and music, it was my dad. When he was younger, dancing to the Big Bands had been his favorite pastime. As he got older he became more sedentary, and looked to the movies for escape. He was happiest when he was watching an old movie with one of his kids, pointing out things the average person never even thought to notice.

Hollywood was everything he had hoped it would be. Not only did we tour the studios, we also visited many landmarks on Hollywood and Vine as well as the homes of the stars. There were guided tours of their residences, but our dad had his own ideas on that; he had mapped out exactly where we would go, which houses we would hit, and what time we would arrive on the scene based on when we were most likely to see the stars. Dad made a color-coded map with handwritten notes and timelines on it, planning our tour to a T. If only the stars had co-operated, we would have seen a dozen or so; as it turned out, we only saw a couple of maids. But, as in everything else my dad did, it was not so much the end result that proved entertaining as the means to the end.

After we had exhausted all possible modes of stargazing in Hollywood, we went to Disneyland. I'm not sure which magical place gave my dad the most happiness, Hollywood or Disneyland. He loved Walt Disney and had studied his drawings with great intensity; in Dad's earlier days he had done quite a bit of cartooning himself, and had even been commissioned to sketch pamphlets for the Barnum and Bailey Circus that came to Memphis every year—a gig he snagged through the influence of my cousin Millie, a well-known artist in Memphis at the time.

We spent a couple of days at Disneyland before traveling north on the Ventura Highway to catch up with my mom and her family in San Francisco. We stayed about a week with my grandmother, visiting all the local sights: Muir Woods, the Golden Gate Bridge, Chinatown, Fisherman's Wharf, the Crookedest Street, and Hate Ashbury. When our visit was over, Mom caught the Greyhound once again and headed for home, as she had to get back to work.

Dad, Steve, and I, on the other hand, with no responsibilities waiting on us back home, began the most memorable vacation imaginable. We went to the Painted Desert, the Carlsbad Caverns, Yosemite, the Redwood Forest, the Grand Canyon, Hoover Dam, Las Vegas, Reno, the OK Corral, Boot Hill, the Navajo Reservation, Lake Tahoe, Salt Lake, the Mormon Tabernacle, the Rockies, Yellowstone, and a hundred other tourist sites along the way. Every day we saw something new and stayed in a different place. It was entertaining and illuminating—and exhausting.

It was almost too much for a nine-year-old to take in. I'm sure my brother remembers far more than I, being six years older, but a few vivid memories have stuck with me over the years. One of these was our hike down the Grand Canyon. Because we were on a tight budget, we did not ride the mules like most families with children; instead, we walked the very narrow trail. It took us all day and all night. I remember being so tired, I thought my legs were going to fall off. When I couldn't go another step, my dad and brother took turns carrying me piggyback all the way to the top.

This obviously slowed us down, and the sun began to set. The path was unlit and steep, and my dad got a little nervous, as there were places where you could fall over the edge and plummet below. The mules had long since made their way back to the stables, and there was only one other couple on the trail: a man, who had fallen and sprained his ankle, supported by his faithful companion just a few yards ahead. A search party was finally sent out after us, and brought flashlights to guide us home. We made our way back to our little trailer at the top of the canyon, all of us bone-weary, and fell into bed in our dirty clothes.

Another vivid memory was the day my dad left us locked in our trailer all day while he went into Las Vegas to gamble. We had parked in a small campsite right outside "Sin City." Dad got up early one morning, showered, shaved, dressed to the nines, and then told Steve and me to stay in the trailer till he got back, locking us in with plenty of food and magazines. He didn't tell us where he was going.

It was suffocatingly hot. Steve opened the windows, even though Dad had told us not to, and we put the fans on full speed, sitting in front of them to try to keep cool. Steve, who was old enough to know what my dad was up to, was very angry about the whole thing, and when Dad finally returned after what seemed like an eternity, the two of them got into a big fight. I can't blame my brother. What my dad did was very wrong, and would probably be considered child abuse today, but dad didn't think a thing about it. He wanted to gamble, and knew he couldn't have us tag along. In his mind we weren't in any danger, but in reality he let his own selfish ambitions cloud his judgment. When Steve confronted him about this, Dad got mad and stormed off—partly to get away from Steve, and partly to escape his own guilt.

My favorite memory is a rather silly one. As we approached the end of our three-month road trip, Steve and I were getting cabin fever and ready to go home. Dad finally decided we'd seen enough, and besides, we were running out of money; so we geared up for our journey back toward the Memphis-Arkansas Bridge. But along the way, somewhere near Oklahoma, we got behind a turkey truck on the interstate, and watched in amazement as a turkey wriggled its way through the wire mesh and escaped, landing right in front of us on the road. We had to swerve to avoid it.

Dad pulled over, and Steve and I cringed, knowing what would happen next. Dad never could walk or drive past a hurt animal. Every time we came across a dog trying to cross the highway, he would stop, pick it up, and carry it to safety; if it was hungry, he would get it food. Most of the time he would bring the animal home, and we would keep it. The mangier the animal, the more compassion it would elicit from Dad; he was the original Animal Rescuer. So Steve and I could see the writing on the wall—or should I say, the trailer.

That turkey was the luckiest bird in western civilization. It took possession of our entire home on wheels for the rest of the trip, because the trailer was unfit for human habitation with the turkey in the back of it, digesting and excreting every bit of food we could find to feed it. Now we *really* longed to see that Memphis-Arkansas Bridge! I could tell Dad was ready to get back as well, because he no longer stopped in every town along the way to inquire about its history and attractions.

Just a few days after picking up the bird we saw the Memphis skyline in the distance, glistening behind the bridge that would take us home. It was late afternoon, and nothing looked more lovely to me than those buildings on the other side of the Mississippi River. As we crossed the bridge, I once again looked down at the tugboats and thought about the sweetness of home. Memphis was not as exciting as San Francisco or Los Angeles, Las Vegas or Reno, but it was where I wanted to be more than any place in the world.

We crossed the bridge and zipped through downtown Memphis with one single purpose in mind: to get home as fast as we could. Steve and I got a little put out when Dad pulled into the Gulf station just minutes from our destination to collect on that bet he'd made with Glen. After pocketing the five dollars Glen owed him, he finally drove down our street. We were the third building from the corner, and the very sight of it gave me goose bumps. I loved our street. I loved our apartment buildings. I loved the tenants and neighbors I had grown up with, and I missed them; I missed my mother and grandmother, too. They came running outside to greet us, and Steve and I were out of the station wagon before Dad could park it. We were so excited to be home and to show off our new pet, Tom Turkey.

Not surprisingly, Grandma wasn't as excited about Tom as we were. Tom stayed with us all of September and October. At first Dad said he was fattening him up for Thanksgiving, but we knew better: Dad had never killed an animal in his life, and we had all grown attached to Tom by now. The turkey had the full run of the big dog pen on the side of the house, and the dog was put elsewhere for the time being.

Tom was enjoying his new life with us when, much to our dismay, we found him dead one morning. We never did find out for sure, but we strongly suspect it was one of the tenants that caused his demise. Mrs. Reeves, the tenant who always complained about the heat, had lodged another complaint: flies! It seemed that Tom was attracting a lot of them. So Mrs. Reeves had taken it upon herself to spray the pen with insecticide, but instead of killing the flies, it killed Tom. We will never know whether Tom would have ended up on our Thanksgiving table, but if Glen had been laying odds, he would have bet not.

Betting on the destiny of a turkey is humorous. Betting as a way of life, not so much. One of the sadder and graver periods in my dad's life was when he had a gambling addiction. He would never have called it an addiction himself; he would have said he had a "system." But it was a system that almost broke up his marriage.

THE GAMBLE

Dad really believed the dog track in West Memphis Arkansas operated according to some sort of mathematical pattern. If he could just figure out the pattern, he'd be able to lay a huge bet, win a lot of money, and be set for life. So he put together a plan. He spent hours and hours developing mathematical patterns and comparing them to the patterns he found on the betting forms left behind by disappointed gamblers.

As usual, he used Steve and me to do the legwork. He would drive us over the bridge to West Memphis, where the Greyhound dogs raced every weekend, and wait till the track closed. Just before the cleanup began, he'd get us to pick up used racing forms so he could study them and discover the winning patterns of each dog. He made each of us a stick with a nail on the end, and sitting on the tailgate of our blue station wagon—the one that had taken us out west—we would use our sticks to poke through the betting forms lying on the ground and pick them up as Dad drove slowly around the parking lot. It was a monotonous job, but it made us feel like we were part of something big whenever Dad told us this would be our ticket to riches.

As I sat on the tailgate of the station wagon I envisioned a big white house and a red convertible car, like the one

Robert Goulet was driving that day in Hollywood. I thought about all the pretty clothes I could buy with the money we were going to win. I thought about how Mom and Grandma wouldn't have to work anymore and could stay home for a change. I thought about all the places we could travel by plane, and how we would stay in real hotels and swim in nice swimming pools. I had my dreams too, and I was going to make sure that when we won the big money I'd get to make them come true.

Dad would take the racing forms home and place them in meticulous order on the dining room table, his usual work station. Writing down the names of all the dogs, the days they won, the days they lost, and the sequence in which each dog placed week after week, he would then find patterns of wins and losses. He made detailed notes on the first, second, and third place winners. When he began to see a winning pattern, he would write it down and test it out.

At first he placed only small bets; once he began to get the results he wanted, he placed bigger ones. It became an obsession with him. He let us go with him to pick up the racing forms, but he went alone to bet on the dogs, upping the ante each time he placed a bet. There was one time, however, when he did let us go with him to an actual race. It was incredible to watch the muscular dogs chase the little electric rabbit. We yelled and cheered as they turned the corner and sprinted past us. It was intoxicating, and I saw how it could easily become a habit.

And that is exactly what happened: my dad formed a habit that was very hard to break. My mom saw what was happening and tried to talk to him about it, asking him to stop, but as is typical with gamblers, he objected to the absurdity of quitting while he was ahead. He hadn't made a big killing yet, but his wins outweighed his losses and he was bringing home a pretty good profit each week—so much so, that he told my mom he wanted to become a professional gambler.

His plan was to take his winning system and travel to other dog tracks in other towns, and then when that proved successful, use his system to win bets on the horse races. His intent was eventually to take his system to an even higher level, and learn the patterns of the casinos in Vegas and Reno, so convinced was he that it could and would work in any gambling situation. It was just a matter of nailing the mathematical pattern, and if anyone could do it, he could.

My mom recently shared with me that this was one of the hardest things she endured in their marriage. She did not want her children growing up with a professional gambler for a father, or growing up breathing the atmosphere of gambling and the underworld. She did not want her family living out of a suitcase as they traveled to places like Reno and Vegas. Little did she know we had already been to those places with our dad during our trip out west.

So when Dad announced this career plan, Mom was beside herself. She and Grandma banded together to try to talk some sense into him, but that just pushed him into a corner and he came out fighting. He wasn't about to let two women tell him what to do with his life! He had found a way to achieve everything he wanted, something that would bring him money and freedom from the blue-collar life he'd been a slave to for the past thirty years. He was designed for a more exciting way of living, and his system was going to get it for him.

Mom let him know that although she had put up with a lot, she would *not* put up with this; she would not stay with him if he continued on this path; however, Dad was too mesmerized by the glitter of the gambling world to take her seriously. For the first time in their marriage, my mom actually stood up to my dad and voiced her objection, and she backed it up with a dead-serious threat of leaving him.

Dad paid no attention. His little pot of winnings continued to grow, and his main source of financial backing came, in fact, from my mom—the very woman who hated his gambling addiction the most. Dad would drive down to where she worked and meet her in the parking lot on her lunch hour, begging for funds. As much as she tried, she could never say no to him. He was very persistent and knew how to manipulate my mom into doing whatever he wanted. She would accompany him to the bank, and withdraw the amount he wanted. This went on for months until he had more than ten thousand dollars, a pretty sizable amount in 1968; it was the equivalent of close to ninety-thousand dollars today. That was huge for our family. It could have bought my mom her own home.

But Dad was not interested in a house. He was interested in using that money to prove that he had what it took to become wealthy through systematic gambling. So after months of successful wins, he decided it was time to place the big bet and rake it in. Donning his finest suit, silk tie, and polished patent leather shoes, he patted on his Old Spice aftershave, tucked his envelope of cash inside his vest pocket, and left for the track before Mom got home from work.

He was gone a very long time. When he came home that night, Grandma met him at the door. He looked like he'd been hit by an eighteen-wheeler. He was leaning against the door frame, bent over, as if he were about to throw up and faint at the same time. Staggering wordlessly into his room, he threw himself on the bed and slept for the rest of the evening and well into the following day. He emerged only to go to the bathroom, returning quickly to retreat under the covers as if to hide from the world.

No one had to tell us what had happened. We knew. Dad had lost every bit of the ten thousand dollars, and then some. My mom would tell you that the loss was a gift from God, for it completely destroyed Dad's gambling addiction and any dreams of a gambling career. My dad never gambled again. The loss that night, although torture for him, was really the saving grace that kept my mom from leaving my dad and breaking up our family. After a couple of weeks of severe depression my dad began to venture out of his room, and eventually he found some new project to occupy his mind. He attacked it with the same mental tenacity he applied to everything else—and, as usual, Steve and I were right in the middle of it, carrying out our dad's wishes and doing the legwork.

The idea of success was very important to my dad. He wanted to achieve something and be somebody, and in his mind this meant acquiring a great deal of money. That is why he gambled. That is why he quit school to sell a product he thought would be the means to his fortune. That is why he did everything he did: it was as if he had to prove himself. He knew he had the intellect, far above that of the average person. He had the looks, the personality, and the charisma. He had a beautiful wife who loved him. But there was some deep-seated privation that caused him to doubt himself, and to feel less than others for his entire life.

THE CURSE

My dad believed in a generational curse. I did not. But I do believe that our parents' decisions and actions can affect us in ways for which we have no control. Such was the case with my dad, whose father had abandoned him. Perhaps, deep down, that abandonment made my dad feel rejected or unloved. Or maybe the fact that his father was absent left him without a male role model to show him important life lessons. What my grandfather did model (when he made the occasional appearance) was irresponsibility, anger, intoxication, manipulation, and selfishness. If there is a generational curse, then this was it.

My grandfather's absence forced my grandmother to work long hours to put food on the table, leaving my dad alone much of the time. I know my grandmother did the best she could under the circumstances, but it's unrealistic to suppose that she came home full of vim and vigor after a day of physical labor. She came home, cooked dinner, washed clothes, bathed herself and the children, and probably collapsed. I doubt there was much energy left for fun and games, or even affection. For a young boy, this kind of environment most likely added to feelings of loneliness and rejection.

Not only do our parents have a great influence on how we see ourselves; almost anyone else we come in contact with can also contribute to our image of self, especially people whose opinion we value, such as friends, employers, or teachers. For someone like my dad, who already had low self-esteem, the harsh words of others had the power to penetrate deep into his soul and stay there.

If he told me the story of his middle school teacher once, he told it a hundred times. That is no exaggeration. Over the course of my life with him I'm sure he mentioned this episode at least a hundred times, which would only be once or twice a year. It was obviously an incident that left an imprint on his mind and heart for the rest of his life, even though it was no more than a simple statement that a teacher made to him when he was in eighth grade.

I don't know what my dad did to provoke the teacher, but whatever it was, it made the teacher so mad that he didn't hesitate to embarrass my dad in front of the entire class. The teacher yelled at him openly in front of everyone and told him he would never amount to anything. That was it. And that was all it took. Up until the very last days of his life, my dad repeatedly recounted that teacher's words, long after the teacher's name was forgotten. And then he would say, "Well, I guess he was right."

It always made me sad to hear my dad say that. I suppose that if my dad had achieved worldly success, he would have been able to say, "Well, I guess he was wrong." But since, in my dad's mind, he was a failure, he believed that the teacher had somehow predicted his future for him, had cursed him. And maybe he did. Maybe those words had more power than anyone really understands. Words are powerful, particularly when the hearer is in an impressionable stage of his life.

I should know; I was the same age when my dad said some things that stayed with me for the rest of my life. The things he said were aimed at my brother, but they made an impression on me, and if they made an impression on me as an onlooker, I can only imagine their impact on Steve. In many ways, my dad did to my brother what that teacher had done to him. I remember Dad telling my brother he would never amount to anything. It was totally uncalled for; my brother was such a sweetheart. But there were times he and Dad disagreed, and if Steve didn't toe the line, Dad would say very hurtful things to him.

Part of Dad's explosive behavior was a by-product of his bipolar cyclical patterns of emotional instability. Part of it was related to his frustration at not being the provider he longed to be. Part of it was his unhappiness with himself, knowing that despite great intellect and talent he could not achieve what he knew he was capable of. Part of it was guilt, because he knew he had lived selfishly while my mother and grandmother did the unselfish and difficult work of making ends meet. But to my mind none of this excused my dad's behavior, and I resented him for it until the last days of his life.

I carried this resentment during my middle school years when I was old enough to understand life a little more. My brother was in high school, and I witnessed a lot of fights and cruel verbal exchanges between him and my dad. I also began to compare my dad to my friends' dads, who all seemed to have regular jobs and go to work every day, and that became a real issue with me. I wanted a dad who got up every morning, showered and shaved, put on a suit, and went to work—not a dad who slept till noon and sat at the dining room table all day making paper plans that never materialized.

My dad became an embarrassment to me. He was then at a stage of his life where he had little self-respect or pride left, and stayed stubble-faced all day in scruffy clothes that smelled of body odor. When he came to pick me up from school or church, I never introduced him to my teachers or friends; I ran to the car quickly, and slunk as low as possible in my seat until we were a block or two away.

My college roomie and best friend Joanna recently told me how she dropped by to visit me one day when she had been in school in Memphis. She knocked on my door, and to her great shock and embarrassment my dad answered in bare-chest and underwear. She was sure she had awakened him with her knocking, even though it was well into the afternoon.

The day she told me this she laughed about it, though apparently too embarrassed to tell me thirty years earlier. It didn't surprise me—except that Dad usually wore boxers, and Joanna insisted these were not boxers. My dad went shirtless most of the time. If he did wear a shirt it was an undershirt (the wife-beater kind), and even that didn't stay on in the summer. Obviously, he dressed more appropriately when leaving home, but he didn't leave home much during my high school and college days. One particular afternoon stands out in mind—one in which I'm sure he wishes he had donned a shirt. Perhaps a bulletproof vest would have served him better.

I had come home from college for the weekend, and as I pulled into the driveway I saw my mom running down the street past the neighbor's front yard. I parked the car, went into the house, and looked for my dad to see what was going on. Dad was not to be found. I decided to try to catch up with Mom, but by the time I got back outside she was nowhere in sight. I ran down to the neighbor's house and asked if they had seen her. Mr. Jackson leaned over his rocking chair and spit a big wad of tobacco in his spittoon before shaking his head up and down.

"I saw your dad chasing two young men, and your mom was chasing your dad with a hammer in her hand," he replied flatly. The Jacksons had lived four houses down from us for as long as I could remember. They sat on their front porch every afternoon from about three o'clock until suppertime.

"Oh, my goodness!" I replied. "What in the world—?"

"We don't know," Mrs. Jackson chimed in. "All we know is that two young men were running very fast, and your father was not far behind them. Your mom was not far behind him. If you hurry, you can probably catch them. Do you want us to call the police?"

"I don't know. I guess not; not yet. Thanks."

"Oh, yeah…one more thing. Your dad was bleeding," Mr. Jackson added dryly. I guess this older couple was no longer surprised by our family's antics. They had seen plenty over the past twenty years.

"Great," I said, rolling my eyes as I picked up my pace.

I caught up with Mom, who had run as far as she could and was trying to catch her breath. Panting, she explained to me what had happened. Apparently Dad had been watering the plants on our front porch while wearing nothing but his khaki work shorts, when these two men approached from nowhere and asked if they could use the phone. At that time all we had was a landline, and Dad was the king of the landline. We had telephone cords that extended for miles, so it was not a problem for Dad to honor their request. He kept a phone on the porch anyway.

They pretended to use the phone, but in reality they were looking for an opportunity to steal his wallet. Dad usually had his guard up, so these guys must have been pretty good at what they did, because Dad relaxed enough to turn his back on them while watering a plant. That was all they needed. The older of the two knocked Dad down and grabbed his wallet out of his back pocket. But before the thief could get away, Dad reached around with his arm and caught him in a headlock up against his chest.

By this time the young kid had fled the scene, leaving his partner in crime to fend for himself. Dad was no wimp; even in his sixties, he was strong, especially if he was angry. And Dad was angry. His adrenaline kicked in, and he started squeezing the guy's neck so hard that the only way the man could get free was to bite his way out.

The next thing Mom heard from inside the house was Dad yelling as the man bit a chunk out of his chest. Dad let go his hold, and the man ran off the porch, leaving the wallet behind. Mom arrived on the scene just in time to see Dad chasing the man down the street. She picked up the hammer lying near the window ledge and took off after them.

"Are you sure you're okay?" I asked my mom with bated breath.

"Yes, I'm fine. But I don't know about your father. He was just a few feet behind them, and I'm afraid of what'll happen if he catches up to them."

"You stay here. I'll try to find him."

"No!" she said firmly. "No sense you getting hurt just because your father thinks he's twenty years old."

Before I could argue with her, we saw Dad turning the corner on his way back home. He looked like a wounded warrior. Covering his breast with one hand and his heart with the other, he made his way back toward us with a smile on his face. He was actually pleased, perhaps that he could still keep up with younger men, or perhaps that the hoodlums didn't get away with his wallet. Or perhaps he was pleased that he never caught them: he'd used all his energy chasing them, and he knew that if he'd caught up to them they would have hurt him more than he could have hurt them.

He was fortunate they were faster. Just a few weeks earlier, a similar incident had occurred not too far from us, when two adolscents grabbed the purse of a young girl. She chased them as my dad had done, and when she caught up to them, they put a bullet through her head. Yes, Les was fortunate that day.

After we stopped the bleeding and bandaged the hole in Dad's chest, we cleaned up the overturned plants on the porch. It looked like a crime scene from NCIS. Dad refused to go to the emergency room; as usual, he treated himself. We seldom went to the doctor in our family, as Dad never thought we had the money. He didn't mind wasting money on outrageous investments, but he refused to spend money on his health.

In any case, with his wound cleaned and dressed, he thought he would be okay, and there was no convincing him otherwise. One thing he was convinced about, however, was that wearing a shirt while working outside was probably a good idea. As far as his attire inside the house…well, that did not change.

Apparently, Joanna didn't get the memo the day she came to visit. Since Dad did not start his day until after noon, the likelihood of finding him fully clothed was remote. Joanna had no idea that when she knocked on the door she would find a real live Archie Bunker on the other side.

Memo: "When visiting the Ash's, make sure you arrive after two in the afternoon, or you will most likely find Les in bare chest and boxers." Or, according to Joanna…briefs!

THE TEMPER

Another embarrassment to me during my middle and high school years was my dad's temper. Our family (and tenant family) had kept the secret of his temper and bipolar disorder through most of my elementary years, but by the time I reached seventh grade his frustrations were mounting, and it was not as easy to contain the secret. By the time I got to high school, Dad was in his late fifties and his unhappiness had reached an all-time high, especially with the death of my grandmother in my junior year. The sadness and loneliness he felt, not to mention the guilt (for not being the son he thought he should have been), surfaced in bouts of depression and in verbal abuse toward both my brother and my mom, and sometimes me.

I fought with him over and over. I cannot remember the specific issues we fought about, but I certainly remember how these verbal exchanges made me feel about him and about myself. In the fallout from one big blowout we had, I decided to leave home and go stay with friends. As I was backing the car down the driveway he came out in his undershirt and boxers, pleading with me not to leave, but I was so mad I couldn't talk to him. He had made me feel small and unlovely too many times, and I needed to get away. I knew he loved me; I couldn't deny that. But I was to the point that I simply could not handle his behavior. I would no longer take the verbal abuse lying down. I guess I was more like my grandmother than like my mother—or maybe I was more like Dad.

I didn't stay away long, but when I came back things were different. I became the thorn in his side, refusing to let him get away with his abusive temper or negative comments. He noticed the change and commented on the fact that I was not the same toward him anymore, that we were not as close as we used to be. The only real difference was that instead of internalizing my feelings, I was expressing them, and he did not like what he heard. His failures had given him an insecurity complex that was magnified by the depression he endured when coming off a manic episode. He began writing poetry about how everyone was against him. He usually made it somewhat humorous, and we all laughed, but it wasn't really funny at all, because deep inside he felt exactly what the poems were saying.

It was about this time that he pretty much gave up on making anything of himself, and decided to put all his hopes into his children. He especially put pressure on my brother, who was a very talented musician and songwriter. Steve had been in a band since he was fourteen, and at age sixteen went on the road with a trailer and "The Funky Down Home Boys." He had several songs recorded at one of the studios downtown, and quite a few important folks in the music business were interested in him. He actually had a single that was played frequently on the radio and reached the top ten for a couple of weeks.

Dad kept the radio on all the time, methodically tracking the airtime the song was getting; years later, after his death, my friend Joanna told a funny story at the graveside of how every radio station in the house would be blaring loudly whenever she came over. In true Les Wilson fashion, he developed a system for calling all the radio stations and enlisted the help of everybody he could to do the calling: neighbors, relatives, tenants, me, and all our friends. He also drove me to all the record shops in town to buy Steve's single (vinyl 45s in paper sleeves); an hour after making a purchase, he'd send me into the same store in different clothes and a cap to buy another copy. We did this over and over again. Steve eventually left Memphis and moved to Los Angeles, where he kept writing and recording and pitching. And Dad kept pushing. He wanted so badly for someone in our household to be famous!

He also wanted someone to be rich. When we went out to Los Angeles to visit Steve in my senior year of college, Dad took my mom and me to try out for the game shows, certain he could win a goldmine on "Name that Tune." Dad knew the melody and lyrics to every song on the planet— every song written before 1970, that is. The only problem was, it was 1980. When the time came to interview for the show, Dad froze; he wanted it too badly, and was overtaken by stage fright. I, on the other hand, was irritated that I had to be dragged along, because I wanted to spend the day at the beach. Dad forced me to attend one of the interviews, and because I couldn't care less, I was at ease and told funny stories about Dad bringing us out to Los Angeles in a duct-tape station wagon from Tennessee. The television scouts loved my sense of humor and my accent, and selected me to be on one of the most popular game shows at the time, Card Sharks.

The game required no intelligence, only luck. I was on for two days but didn't make it to the big money till the second day. Even though I got close to winning, it wasn't in the cards—and my dad, sitting in the audience with my brother and mom, just couldn't take it. Letting his anger get the best of him, he walked out right in the middle of my show and fumed all the way back to Steve's apartment. I was a big hit and having a ball, but instead of enjoying the moment with me he got frustrated that things weren't turning out as he had hoped. What could have been a really fun day turned out to be yet another one in which I felt I had let him down. There would be many of those days.

As we got older, and Steve and I each had our own families, we would all get together for the holidays and special occasions. Dad would start out fairly decent, but before the visit was over he would usually be pouting somewhere in a corner because he felt that no one was paying him any attention. If he got interrupted while speaking, he would fold his hands across his chest, look down at his feet, and stay in that position for an hour. We could never tell if he was really upset, putting on an act, or manipulating us to get the attention he desired. My brother, who couldn't stand to see him in this state, usually gave in and appeased him. I ignored it. I was just too tired of the game.

My son, Michael, also tended to ignore his grandfather, and had done so ever since he was a toddler. It frustrated my dad to no end that he couldn't get Michael to hug him for very long or show affection toward him. Michael had a connection with my mom, but not so much with my dad; he was a sensitive child, and perceived something overbearing about my dad that didn't sit well with him. Michael loved his grandfather, but didn't have the patience for him, nor did he care if Dad knew it. Michael's bond with Mom only made it all the harder for him to appreciate the grandfather who belittled her. But he kept his antipathy for Dad to himself most of the time—until after he married.

By the time Michael and Melody married, Dad was much older and in poor health. He was also on the other side of the state, and visits were few and far between. Melody had been in an abusive marriage before she met Michael, and knew first-hand what manipulation looked like in its worst form. She had survived her first marriage by learning how to detach herself from the emotional havoc abusers wreak on their victims. Melody could see how manipulative and abusive my dad was, but she never got to experience the generous and caring man who deeply loved his family; by the time she and Michael married, Dad had grown childish, often sullen and easily irritated. Both of them pretty much steered clear of him.

Melody, however, was able to be more objective and probably saw the situation in its truest light. The rest of us had been co-dependent for so long, we usually excused Dad or tried to appease him just to keep the peace. One day Melody showed me a book that had been written to help victims of abuse find healing and live normal lives, saying she thought it might help me. I was surprised; I didn't realize I needed healing. I didn't realize, till that moment, that I had been a victim.

LIFE AFTER LES

THE CLOSET OF SECRETS

Once again Dad had said some pointedly hurtful things that had ignited feelings in me I couldn't control, feelings of hostility and contempt. Dad was in his nineties at the time and still very much in control of his environment, although he protested constantly that he was not. He was still in control of all the people who surrounded him, especially my mother, my brother, and me. I don't remember the exact details of the incident that provoked my negative feelings, but I know I felt manipulated, which led to further feelings of defeat, frustration, and anger (the usual pattern).

I began talking about this when I was visiting Melody and Michael in their home. After several minutes of my nonstop chatter, Michael walked out of the room, which was his typical response. Melody, however, continued to listen as I rambled on about the need to forgive my dad and move forward. But when she asked me what I meant by forgiveness, I didn't really know how to answer her. She gave me the book *Mending the Soul*, by Steven Tracy, and told me she thought it would help me. It was a book her counselor had recommended, and she had found it to contain some valuable insights. I graciously accepted the book, put it in my suitcase, and never opened it—until after my dad passed away.

At his death, I went through a somewhat ambiguous grieving process. I was glad Dad was no longer in pain, and I was glad my mother would no longer have to ignore her own needs to take care of his. I was glad my brother would have relief from the constant tirades, and I was glad my sister-in-law would be freed from the overwhelming stress caused by my dad's self-centered behavior. I was glad I would no longer have to feel guilty for not being and doing everything he wanted me to be and do, but I was sad he was gone.

I experienced a gamut of emotions: relief, grief, guilt, peace, hope, sadness, loneliness, disappointment, loss, emptiness, pity, and despair. Most of all I felt a need to forgive. Remembering the book Melody had given me, I skimmed through it trying to find the chapter on forgiveness. But before I came across that chapter, I found one on shame, and that piqued my interest. I took the book to my room, crawled under the covers of my king-size bed, propped the book on my knees, and started reading.

As I read, I found myself identifying with many of the people in the book, especially the victims of verbal abuse and manipulation. Tracy described the shame experienced by victims of this kind of abuse. He also talked a great deal about sexual abuse—something I had experienced as well, although not from my father. The more I read about the shame of sexual abuse, especially in children, the more I realized I had been affected by a secret, which had come back to haunt me forty years later when I had fallen into a pit of despair and depression. Ironically, the depression was perhaps the best thing that could have happened to me, because it forced me to dredge up the subconscious feelings of my past by opening my closet of secrets, so that I could deal with them once and for all.

The first thing I needed to admit was that I carried shame. There were lots of reasons for my shame, but some of it stemmed from an incident outside my control. At a young age I had been sexually molested. I never told anyone. Maybe it was because I didn't think they would believe me; I was just a child, and the man who had molested me was my dad's age, but it probably had more to do with the fact that I felt somewhat responsible. Instead of revolting, I submitted. Furthermore, I was so young I didn't know how to define it, much less understand the implications of such an act.

I had been raised in a very safe environment, sexually speaking. My family life might have been dysfunctional, and my dad certainly had many faults, but he was quite protective of me when it came to anything related to sex. Even though my father was abusive verbally, I was fortunate that I did not suffer in the way that so many other little girls did, whose fathers or stepfathers abused them sexually.

I was not so fortunate, however, when it came to relatives. My uncle was a drunk. One Saturday afternoon when I went to visit my aunt, my uncle came to the door, and greeted me by picking me up so that my face was directly across from his own. He pulled my body tight against his bulging belly, and I felt the crunch of the cigarettes in his shirt pocket. He pressed his nose against mine—and then he kissed me with mouth wide open. I did not know what a French kiss was at the time, but I quickly learned. The whiskey on his breath made the kiss even more unbearable. His three-day stubble scratched my cheeks, and the tongue that he forced between my teeth felt thick and hot. I almost threw up in his mouth. He must have sensed it, and put me down. I ran into the house and washed my mouth out, but said nothing to my aunt.

I had been raised to respect and honor my elders. Mostly, I was too embarrassed to speak of the incident. I was only eight years old, but I knew enough to be aware that what he had done was shameful. The sad part was that for some reason I was the one who felt shame, as if I had invited his actions. I didn't want anyone to know, so I just kept it to myself. I also kept my distance from my favorite aunt's husband until the day he died. Although the act of kissing me was not considered a sexual offense, the way he did so certainly smacked of something unnatural and dirty between an uncle and a niece. I don't know if what my uncle did was the precursor to something more that he hoped to secure from me in the future, or if it was just a one-time impulsive act committed in a drunken stupor. Probably the latter, as he was not the calculating type; I don't think he was that intelligent…but there was another uncle who was that smart, and he would be the one to take it much further.

My grandmother came from a large family and had many brothers and half-brothers from one father and his three wives; Grandma's dad had been widowed twice and remarried both times. The extended family was so large that I couldn't keep up with it. We gathered once a year at one of my uncles' farms for a family reunion, but I didn't know half the people there. Of course, I was young, and all I cared about was the food.

I probably had a hundred cousins ranging from my age to late sixties. It was always confusing to me to figure out whether a cousin was my second, third, or fourth, and how many times removed. To keep it simple, if my cousin was over thirty I called him or her Uncle or Aunt, as I had been taught to do. Most of my relatives were very decent, hard-working people, good citizens who went to church and had wholesome values. But as in every family, there were a few who lived on the dark side. One of these was my "Uncle" Fred. The funny thing was that no one knew he lived on the dark side except me—and I found out the hard way.

One Friday afternoon when my dad was away on a "sales" trip, my Uncle Fred decided to pay us a visit. My grandmother was the only one home as my mom was at her steady nine-to-five job at the Board of Education, and my brother had gone to the church to practice with his band. I had just come home from school and was sitting at the kitchen table doing homework. After exchanging a few niceties, Fred sat down beside me, and Grandma cut him a piece of pound cake.

Grandma was very hospitable; she always kept a freshly baked cake and a pot of coffee on the stove ready for any relative who might drop by for a chat. Uncle Fred said she made the best pound cake in town, and I had to agree; Grandma's made-from-scratch pound cake was to die for. Maybe that was why Uncle Fred was so nice that day: he just wanted more pound cake. I would soon find out there was another reason, but at the time I thought nothing of it; I received a lot of attention from most of my uncles. They thought I was cute and entertaining; they loved to tease me, and I loved being teased.

The difference, however, was that Fred had not been to our home as often as my other relatives, and I didn't know him as well. In fact, the only other time I recalled having seen him was at the picnic the previous weekend. Perhaps he had visited Grandma when I had been at school, as it was not unusual for Grandma's kin to come by at any time of day without an invitation. In her family, you just dropped by and everyone was expected to stop whatever they were doing and play host—something my grandmother did better than anyone.

Most of the time her relations did bring a gift, however, and Fred had brought tomatoes and cucumbers, for which Grandma was extremely grateful. He also brought news of relatives, which tickled Grandma to death. She loved her family, and loved hearing all the details of their comings and goings, and Fred was a good storyteller who gave her plenty of what she wanted. He was quite affable, and I kind of liked him. He had a nice smile.

After finding out about Fred's mom and dad and catching up on all the other kinfolk, Grandma got up from the table to pour us another cup of coffee. She always let me drink coffee when relatives came over, which made me feel very grown up. Uncle Fred began to ask me questions about school, and since I loved school, I was happy to tell him. I was struggling with some of my math homework, however, which was not my strong suit, and Fred was quick to tell me he'd been a math major and would be glad to offer his services. Grandma asked him if he had the time to stay a bit and help me. She needed to check on one of the elderly tenants in 1199, the building across the driveway, and would only be gone a few minutes. It wasn't like her to leave company just to check on a tenant, but Mrs. Raines had called and asked her to come and pick up the rent money before supper. Grandma was a good business woman, and not one to let money matters linger.

I was not happy at the prospect of entertaining Uncle Fred all by myself. Given the way Grandma liked to talk, I knew her few minutes would be more like thirty. Fred seemed nice, of course, but I didn't really know how to converse with him. I looked up at Grandma and rolled my eyes, which only elicited a stern look in my direction; I was expected to be hospitable and friendly to all our relatives, even those I didn't know well. When Fred said he'd be glad to help me, Grandma told him how much she appreciated it, and then instructed me to mind my manners and make sure I did what he said. She untied her apron, picked up the apple pie she had made for our tenant, and headed out the back door.

Her departure was followed by a strange and embarrassing silence. I smiled sheepishly at Fred, and then looked straight down at my paper trying to avoid eye contact and conversation. Fred chuckled, helping to defuse an awkward situation, and pulled his chair close. He showed me a few impressive tricks about my math, and then told me a couple of school stories from his past, which made me laugh.

I was just beginning to relax and enjoy his company when he asked if I minded if he took another piece of cake. "Of course," I said; but he just sat there, so I figured he wanted me to get up and serve it to him. I was used to that, having already been conditioned to the fact that the men in our family expected to be waited upon. I got up and walked over to the counter beside the stove where Grandma had left the cake, but before I could pick it up, I felt a presence directly behind me.

The next thing I knew, Fred had wrapped his arms around me. He told me I was a "pretty little thing," that he had noticed me at the picnic last weekend, and was surprised at how much I had grown. At first I thought he was just being overly affectionate, as some of my uncles were known to be; but things got a little eerie when he whispered in my ear that my hair smelled good, squeezing me tighter with each premeditated syllable.

The dress I was wearing was thin cotton, cheaply made, but cool enough for the hot days at a school with no air conditioning. It was a bit short on me, because of my long legs; my mom did not have the money to buy me more expensive dresses made of better material. Taking advantage of my cheap attire, my uncle slipped his hands into the two front pockets of my dress, below my belly button, and pressed hard against my lower abdomen. Because I was thin, my hip bones protruded; he began rubbing on the inside of my bones, inching closer and closer to my pubic area. He then slid his hands under the material of my dress and felt between my legs, where he rubbed up inside me with long fingers. My loose cotton panties were worn and thin, and he took advantage of that, too.

His breath was hot and labored; I wanted to pull away, but I was frozen and silent. I felt transported into another dimension, stranded on the ledge of a cliff. I closed my eyes; I could not breathe. With smothering arms he pulled me tighter into himself as he pushed his hardness up against my body. I was ten, he was forty, big and strong and commanding. He was my uncle, and he was my elder, so I did nothing but stand there and wait for it to be over.

The ordeal probably lasted no more than a few minutes, but for me time stood still. He released his hold and left. I didn't know what to do. I didn't want to tell my Grandmother; she might not believe me. I didn't want to tell my dad; he was too volatile, and he was my dad. Only my mom would understand. I went to my room and waited for her to come home.

Grandma didn't come to check on me when she returned from Mrs. Raine's apartment. I imagine Fred had made it a point to catch up with her to adequately explain his abrupt departure. I didn't know and I didn't care. When Mom got home she came to my room and we sat and talked. I didn't tell her everything; I didn't want to relive the ordeal by answering a lot of questions; but I told her enough that she made sure I would never have to see my uncle again. Neither my grandmother nor my dad ever talked to me about the incident. I had not relayed every detail, and perhaps my mom, knowing my dad's nature, had relayed even less. All I know is that Uncle Fred never stepped foot in our house again.

I was too young at the time to understand, but Fred was obviously a sexual predator who knew how to skillfully manipulate a situation, including keeping it hush-hush. He knew how to pick his prey. Perhaps he had observed me at the picnic, and saw something in me that he knew he could take advantage of without reprisal. Perhaps he sized me up once he came to our house, and decided that I was not strong enough to fend him off physically or emotionally. Perhaps he sensed in me a submissive spirit, or perhaps he just took a chance. Whatever the case, it was a bold move, and one I am sure he had made many times before. He was just too good at it.

Fred had arrived at our house without notice, bearing gifts of farm table delights. He had charmed us with his seemingly sincere compliments, and put us at ease with his winsome smile and carefully crafted stories. He had known just what to say and when to say it. During the perpetration he had made sure I couldn't face him, or look into his eyes, making it easier for him to do something despicable to the granddaughter of the woman who had trusted him. After the act, he made sure he fed Grandma just the right information to keep her from asking pointed questions. He had known how to make an entrance, and he knew how to make his exit.

I put that day behind me the best I could. I was only ten years old, but I had already learned how to push unwanted memories behind a wall of forgetfulness. At an early age I perfected the technique of conscious removal of negative feelings, and learned to store them in a subconscious vault. That was the way I had managed to keep my sanity in a home where explosives were set off every other week. It was the only way I could put my arms around my dad and kiss him goodnight when I went to bed. It was the only way I could leave my home in the morning, and be around friends all day who had no idea the hurt and pain I experienced in their absence; and as I learned that afternoon, it was the way my mom had learned to survive as well. Much to my surprise, my mom knew how to keep secrets too.

THE LEFT OVERS

I had learned the art of denial, and I used it to my advantage. I looked forward to getting away from secrets, from the tumultuous life on Vance Street, and to the way growing up with a bipolar dad made me feel. When I left home to go to college, I thought everything would be okay. I was now in control of my own destiny, and I was free.

What I didn't realize was that the shame I had felt living at 1191 Vance Street did not stay at 1191 Vance Street. It was packed away in the suitcase of my hidden psyche, and traveled with me everywhere I went. That shame prevented me from seeing myself as someone who was "enough."

Not seeing my self as someone who was "enough" was not a new thing for me. I had fought the feeling even as a child; even before my great aunt's drunken husband pressed me against his belly; even before my Uncle Fred molested me, and even before I kept my dad a secret as a teenager. Even as a six year old, I knew the difference between the girls who were enough, and the girls, like me, who were not. Never was it more evident than the Thanksgiving when all the relatives came to our house for dinner.

Thanksgiving in November and the annual Ash reunion in July were the two big events in our large extended family. Most of the time the July gathering took place at my Uncle John's farm. Every family brought pot luck, and placed it on three long tables positioned end to end in the dining area of the large two-story farmhouse. After dinner there was fishing, croquet, paddle boats, badminton, football for the older boys, and frog gigging for the younger ones. The older folks just sat around and talked while they nibbled on left-overs.

My favorite pastime was sitting in the porch swing and watching all the people. I never cared for fishing, and I thought the spearing of frogs quite cruel, so I usually found myself babysitting some of the younger kids while the older ones got to play. Sometimes my great grandmother would sit on the porch with me and chew tobacco while she knit. Every now and then she forgot which side of her rocker the spittoon was on, and the spittle would land in her bag of yarn; after all she was just one year shy of a hundred. It was easy to keep up with her age, because we always celebrated her birthday during this event. Although sometimes forgetful, she still had her wits about her, as well as her sense of humor, and would tell me funny stories about my dad.

One of her favorite stories about "Leslie" as she called him, was when he was just a toddler. I could always tell when she was getting ready to tell me a "doozy," because she'd lean over the arm of the chair and spit into the copper pot. She'd then wipe the brown leftover wet from her chin, and relax her posture with a quiet chuckle. She knew she had a captured audience, so she took her time recounting dad's antics. She described with delight how he'd waddle down to the train tracks in nothing but his cloth diaper and a slice of white bread in each hand. Once at the tracks, he would crumble the bread and push it down into his diaper as the train passed by, so both hands would be free to wave at the conductor in the caboose. (Even at an early age my dad was fascinated with trains.) By the time he made his way back to the house shared by several relatives, his diaper would be full and soggy and hanging down to his knees. He would then reach into his diaper, pull out the left-over mush, and feed it to his faithful dog, Jack. Granny, as we called her, would then end the story the same way she had started it. She'd lean over the arm of the rocker and aim for the pot.

I can't really say the July reunion was something I dreaded; maybe knowing I'd get a little one on one with Granny helped, but it wasn't really something I looked forward to either. The family was too big, and there were too many relatives, most of whom were direct descendants of Uncle John, my grandmother's step brother. I felt like an outsider. I think my dad did as well. He probably brought some of that on himself, when he tried buttonholing them into signing up as one of his downline in his multi-level networks. Needless to say, his ego took a beating when they teased him about his failed ventures. And of course, when they teased my dad, they might as well have been teasing me. It was painful to see him laughing it off, knowing full well that it was killing him on the inside, and only deepening his already insecure state.

Thanksgivings were better because host sites were divided between my grandmother, her sister, Nell, and their brother, Jordan. These were grandma's full brother and sister, the daughter and son of the mother who died shortly after giving birth to my dad's mom. Again, everyone brought a dish, but the menu was more carefully planned out to ensure we had plenty of turkey and ham to feed all the hungry siblings and their families. The Thanksgiving I remember best was the one we hosted at 1191 Vance. It was also the Thanksgiving I got a spanking I'll never forget.

The spanking was deserved; I had acted out. I was six years old, but I was already feeling like I did not measure up…at least not compared to my third cousin, Becky. Becky was the daughter of my second cousin, Leonard, who was my Aunt Nell's only son, and the son of the drunken ex-sailor who later stuck his tongue in my mouth. Leonard was my dad's first cousin and closest playmate. But when Becky came to our house that Thanksgiving morning, Becky was my enemy. Why I saw Becky as my enemy I really don't know, but I think it had something to do with the relationship between her dad and my dad, and her grandmother and mine.

Grandma and Nell were best friends in their later years, but as young girls there was quite a bit of a rivalry between the two. Both sisters shared the same mom and dad, the same bedroom, and sometimes the same beau. Nell was the prettier of the two, and she knew it. She was quite a bit taller than my shorter more round-bellied grandmother. She had nice long legs, and a figure to match the pretty clothes she liked to wear. When the soldiers came to town, it was usually Nell who won the honor of the date, while Grandma got the left-overs.

I thought about my grandmother and the left-over boys Aunt Nell had conceded to her; then I thought about my dad, and the left-overs he had conceded to us. There was one vivid memory in particular that came to mind. I remembered standing next to my dad as he postured himself in front of the medicine cabinet hanging above our bathroom sink, and I wondered where he was going. I stared up at the hairy-chested man in the wife beater undershirt, and watched with amazement the meticulous grooming regimen he employed every Thursday evening. He would open the cabinet, and pull out a white ceramic cup containing a shaving brush that poked its head above the rim, exposing the badger bristles stuffed in the antique ivory handle.

For as long as I could remember my dad had owned this shaving set, and it had served him well. He would soak the bristles in warm water before vigorously working the soft soap into a lather that he swirled across the entire bottom half of his face. He would use the left hand to lift the cheek skin as the right hand guided the single edge stainless steel razor. Right cheek, left cheek, chin, and then the lifting of the nose tip, giving him plenty of room to maneuver above his lip.

It was fun to watch my dad shave. The razor reminded me of a sled gliding across heaps of white snow. Sometimes he would let me paint his face with the lather, and skim it off with a blade-free razor. Thursdays were the days I could enjoy this simple pleasure with my dad. It was the only day of the week the bathroom door stayed open. When the bathroom door was closed, we knew better than to disturb the king who sat on his throne; if we needed to go, we would have to go outside. Once a day Dad picked up the Commercial Appeal and headed to his plumbed office, where he would spend an hour and a half with paper in hand. But on Thursdays, his office became his barber shop, and the smells were much more pleasant.

After the razor had done its job, he would take a warm towel and wipe away the left-over lather, reach for the Old Spice located on the top shelf of the cabinet, and apply it vigorously to the baby smooth skin before gently slapping both sides of his face, smiling into the mirror, and checking each profile position ensuring his Dapper Dan image. He whistled as he worked, he was happy; he was always happy when he was getting ready to go out on Thursday nights. I didn't know or care where he went; I just knew he smelled good, and when he bent down to kiss me goodbye, felt good as well. It was a nice treat, because most of the time he did neither when he closed in for some affection.

The good night kisses were the worst. I was expected to hug and kiss each parent before bedtime every night. The peck on the cheeks of grandma and mom were painless and quick. My dad was a different story. When I'd lean over to put my arms around him, he'd pull me down into his lap bringing my face to his as he snuggled me into his chest. His three day stubble scratched my cheek, and the stale breath of the puckered kiss was not pleasant. He tried to hold me in that position for several minutes, and always got mad when I squirmed away more quickly than he wanted. This was the nightly routine six evenings a week, every night but Thursday.

I later learned from my brother that Thursday nights had been reserved for jitterbugging. Gen went on the occasion, but most of the time Les went stag; and he probably had a slew of partners to pick from; he was known for his good dancing and charismatic personality. Maybe he had a regular partner; he often talked about his good friend, Mavie. I didn't understand much about what happened on Thursday night, but what I did understand was that had my dad shaved and smelled as good for us as he did for Mavie, I might have wanted to snuggle a little longer in his lap. I might have wanted to rub my cheek against his, and hold him tight, but that wasn't the case. Mavie got the clean shaven "dancing cheek to cheek" Les and we got the leftovers.

And Grandma got the left-overs, as well. There was one glorious week, however, that she got first pick of the young men who came to court. Aunt Nell had gone to visit a relative and do a little shopping, and while she was away, Grandma caught the eye of a strapping "would-be" fireman with whom she enjoyed several dates before Nell returned from her holiday. Once home, however, it didn't take the fireman long to notice the tall, elegant, sophisticated sister, and Grandma knew in her heart it was only a matter of time before she would lose out to Nell again. Sure enough, Nell had a date with the young man the following Saturday after her return, and wore the new black patent leather heels she had bought on her trip.

That night was long and lonely for my grandmother, as she waited for her sister to return from her date with the man she had snatched from her bosom. She went upstairs to the bedroom she shared with her, and watched out the window for her return. She sat on the edge of her bed, chin resting on her palms, feet pumping up and down in agitation, until finally she decided she was wasting her time. She slipped under the covers and made herself go to sleep. She awoke in the middle of the night when she felt the presence of her sister beside her. She didn't know when Nell came in, but she was immobile and immovable.

The clapboard house that Grandma and Nell lived in with their dad and stepmom was not well insulated, making it a wee bit chilly on a cold winter night; but it was nothing compared to the frigid outdoor bathroom located ten yards from the back door. It was not the most enjoyable experience to venture into icy sheets of wind when visiting the outhouse in a cotton thin bed shirt and slippers. So, when Grandma woke up in the middle of the night in great need of relieving herself, she took one look at Nell, another look at the patent leather shoes lying beside the bed that Nell had worn on the date, and she made her decision. She picked up one of the shoes, and placed it strategically between her feet as she squatted over and filled it to the black leather brim. She then quietly returned to her sister's side in the double bed they shared, and enjoyed the best night's sleep she had had in a long time.

Grandma had exacted her revenge, not that she was a revengeful person; the fact is my grandmother was one of the most forgiving people I knew. But I suppose that night she decided it was time to do a little something for Bernice, and being the pragmatic that she was, it made complete and logical sense to save herself from a cold trip to the outhouse. I don't know how my great aunt responded the next morning when she stuck her foot in a shoe full of yellow liquid. I imagine there was much name calling and hair pulling. Grandma never said. But it was a story we all heard more than once; a story which just perhaps planted a seed that began another rivalry for a different generation.

When Dad and Leonard were middle school boys, Leonard was the mean one of the two. Dad would tell me tales of Leonard's bullying ways; how Leonard would make fun of him and beat him up just for the pleasure of it. During those adolescent years, my single-mom grandmother was raising dad alone, while Leonard had both parents at home. Back then there was more of a stigma associated with single moms than there is today.

Once when Leonard was making fun of my grandmother and her absent husband, my dad got mad and pushed his cousin to the ground. Leonard responded by pulling a pocketknife from his pants, and in the mayhem of the scuffle cut my dad on the arm. The blood ended the fight, and both boys went home to clean up and change before their moms found out. The superficial cut did little damage on the outside; the cut to the soul went much deeper.

When telling me the stories, Dad would laugh and shake his head; how ironic that such a brutal little boy could have turned into such a nice man. Grown Leonard had met and married the love of his life at the Methodist church, and the two of them raised a family of four, supported by a highly successful printing business, of which Leonard was the sole proprietor. He became both a deacon and a Sunday school teacher, respected husband and father, and a good provider for his family and his mom, who he visited every Saturday. His mild manner and soft speech only added to the irony of the lives of these first cousins. As much as I hated to admit it, Leonard had turned into a stellar citizen; while my Dad, who had started out as the charming apple of everyone's eye, became the man with the brutal temper and knife-stabbing vocabulary.

Although I liked Leonard and enjoyed his calm demeanor, I always knew that somewhere down inside of him was a mean little boy who had said and done some very hateful things to my father. And the fact that he was so successful only added to the resentment, not that I really cared about all the things he and his family had accumulated; but the fact that Leonard enjoyed a feeling of accomplishment, and I knew that my dad did not. I knew that Thanksgiving morning when I overheard my mom consoling my dad, and I knew that Leonard's presence would only be a reminder to my dad that he lived in the world of the "have nots."

So when Leonard, and his wife, and his four very prim and proper, not to mention, well-dressed children arrived at our home that Thanksgiving morning with turkey in hand, I could not be a grateful pilgrim. I took one look at Becky with her Shirley Temple curls and her pink gingham dress, and I wanted to push her to the ground the way my dad had pushed her dad thirty years earlier. Instead, I invited her out back to play. Once outside, however, when she started acting a little too prissy for her white eyelet britches, and turned her nose up at our "smelly" dog, I could take it no longer. I called her over to the oak tree, and once behind the tree, I looked her square in the eyes and spit in her face.

Needless to say I got a spanking that day, not later that night, not after company left, but right then and there in front of everyone. Les had to show Leonard that he might not be the successful business man he was, but he knew how to raise his children. He knew how to make them mind, and he knew how to punish a heinous crime. My dad took me to the back of the house and pulled out his flat hairbrush. To my relief, he paddled me softer than I was expecting, and then he smiled and said, "good job."

Whatever the reason behind the exhortation, in that moment my dad became my champion, even if it was behind closed doors. He didn't stay on his white horse long, however, and the next day he had another manic episode concerning a deal gone wrong with one of the visiting relatives. The same woman who had tenderly comforted him the morning before was now the recipient of his abusive tongue. The verbal barrage continued into the afternoon, until my dad slammed the door behind his exit and left the house. Who knows where he went, but wherever it was, he probably offered up his best while we got the left-overs. By the time Monday rolled back around all was forgotten, and Gen went back to work: I went out to play.

BULLIES AND SPORTS

I had always been athletic; it was an area in which I excelled. As a young girl I played neighborhood street sports with the kids on the block, most of whom came from one household, the Chins. The Chin family consisted of Edward, the elder son, Bernice, his A-type sister, Lily, the cute little baby girl of the family, and a set of twin boys, Frank and William. They were so identical, that the only way to tell them apart was to look for a small birthmark on the left side of William's face. Their personalities were quite different, however, as William was the angry one, and Frank was the charmer. I had to walk on eggshells around William, but with Frank I could be myself and have a good time. They were like two different people with one face… kind of like my dad. In fact, I learned how to deal with the twins especially well, because I had had so much experience with my own father.

The Chins were my constant playmates. We did everything together. We played street football, church yard baseball, kickball, kick the can, and spy games. We sat on the front steps every night of the summer telling funny stories and jokes. When the twins had to run a paper route to help with expenses, I rode on the back of the bike and folded the papers. The time I spent with the Chin boys set the stage for my athleticism and confidence in sports. The twins were my best friends until I reached adolescence my seventh grade year, and was sent to a school across town that did not bus in black students. My mom worked at the Board of Education, and begged her boss, at the insistence of my dad, to pull some strings and have me transferred to an all white school out east. I did not want to go. I loved my neighborhood, and had been very happy at Bruce Elementary where Eddie the Cop walked me across the busy intersection on my way to school every morning.

After the shooting of Martin Luther King in downtown Memphis, my dad lived in fear of a black uprising. He had a fear of the black community, not individual black people, just the community at large. He had watched, as we all did, the riots and mayhem that took place on the main streets of Memphis, and the businesses that were destroyed and looted in protest of Dr. King's murder. The Chin family, who owned a Sundry in the downtown area, took a big hit; their shop was looted several times, and the dad had been threatened. Had it not been for a large Chinese population that came to their aide, they would have lost their store. I had been too sheltered to understand the reasons behind it all; what I did understand was the assassination of Dr. King was horrible, and would change everything. A man of peace had been shot, and there would be peace no more…at least not for a very long time.

There was certainly no peace for me. I begged my dad not to send me to a different school. When my schoolmates found out about the transfer, they turned against me. They saw me as someone who thought better of herself than her friends, someone who no longer wanted to be a part of them, and they systematically disconnected themselves from me little by little; I became an outsider in the very neighborhood I had once ruled.

I hated East High School. It was four times larger than Bellevue Junior High, my neighborhood school, where all my friends were going. It boasted of an elementary school, junior high and high school all in one massive building. The school and number of students was overwhelming, but the worst part was getting up an hour earlier and riding a diesel driven stop and go city bus everyday. Not only did I choke on the diesel, I choked on the cigarette smoke embedded in the clothes of other passengers, whose open eyes I never saw. I did make one friend, named Monica, who like me was being made to go to a school she detested by a parent who was scared of integration. Monica had a friend named Cynthia, and together we formed an unlikely trio to stave off the bullies at East Junior High. And there were plenty of bullies; never was this more evident than when the unsupervised cafeteria opened its doors at eleven forty-five every morning.

School cafeterias are the worst, and East Junior High was no different than any other school. We knew better than to sit at the table with the cheerleaders, so we found one near the back. Little did we realize we had chosen a table next to the degenerates of the school. We had the table to ourselves, but the one behind us boasted of older boys with joints concealed in the rolled up sleeves of their shirts. The girls at the table were loud and scrappy looking. There was one girl in particular who did not like me. I don't know why. I had always said hello and been nice; maybe that was the problem. Whatever the case, she had it out for me.

I'll never forget her face. She had frizzy red hair that barely touched her shoulders, and her cheeks were covered with freckles so thick you could hardly see the pale white skin that lay beneath. She was not unattractive, just unusual looking. She typically dressed in jeans with a tank top layered under a long sleeve flannel shirt. She looked tough, and sounded even tougher. I don't know that I was actually afraid of her. I could have probably taken her; but I wasn't built that way, and I didn't have a gang of bully boys sitting at my table to back me up.

Once you found a table, you pretty much stuck with it, as the other tables were usually occupied by their particular groups and cliques: cheerleaders, football players, artists, thespians, skaters, science nerds, misfits, potheads, bullies and then us…the newbies. It was no use looking for another table. There wasn't a day to go by that the Redhead didn't have a derogatory remark to make about me. She would make fun of my clothes, my purse, my shoes, and my accent. She made fun of my friends as well, but seemed to take a special interest in me.

Every afternoon, on the way to the bus stop, I had to pass her and her friends smoking pot around the corner of the school building; she always yelled some obscenity which made my skin crawl. The worst day of my life at East, however, was when her brother caught me on the steps in-between classes, and took great pleasure in flipping up my skirt, exposing my panties for all the other bully boys to see and enjoy. She and her brother, and their friends, made my life miserable for the first three months at East Junior High.

I talked to my dad about it. I wanted him to bring me back to my neighborhood school. He was adamant. His pride kept him from admitting he had made a wrong decision; his fear kept him from allowing us to face an unknown future in a school that had a different demographic than what he was ready for. He had made a judgment call, and I needed to be good with it. I told Mom how miserable I was, and begged her to plead with Dad to let me go to Bellevue. She said her boss had done us a great favor by getting me the transfer, and I needed to finish the year, but that she would talk to my father about attending Bellevue for eighth grade.

I went back to East after Christmas with a new attitude. I needed to hang in there for just four more months. My dad had told me to be nice to the girl and things would get better. My dad knew nothing about female bullies. I had been nice, and it had only made things worse. I decided to try a different approach. The next time the Redhead belittled me, I looked directly into her eyes, didn't blink, and told her in no uncertain terms that if she kept messing with me, I would be glad to take it outside. She never bothered me again. The four months flew by, and the following year I was back at my neighborhood school with my friends, and a black and white student ratio of fifty-fifty. I loved every minute of it.

When I graduated from junior high, I attended Central High School, the neighborhood school that was three houses away from my alarm clock. I could wake up to the seven forty-five bell, and be in my homeroom seat by the time the eight o'clock bell quit ringing. I lettered in both tennis and basketball. My dad was pleased that I had joined the tennis team. Even as a little girl, he had tried to teach me different aspects of the game. He was in love with Chris Evert, and if I couldn't grow up to be Rita Hayworth, maybe I could be another Chrissie. He would take me to the Beauregard Tennis Center close to downtown, and work with me on fundamentals, showing me how to hold the racket with a continental grip, how to put my left foot forward when hitting a forehand, my right foot forward when hitting a backhand, and how to pick up a ball with my foot. Very old school compared to today, but it was how

Jimmy Conners and Chrissie Evert did it, and that was all that mattered.

I loved tennis, and felt very pretty in the white tennis dress with ruffled panties that my mom made for me with her Singer sewing machine. I didn't have the fancy store-bought tennis outfit the other girls had, but I had the cutest. I did well at tennis, and won quite a few matches. I never had a lesson, except for the ones my dad gave me; but my mom, who had won the City tournament in San Francisco during high school, was my biggest inspiration. She worked with me on strategy and serving. Mostly, she encouraged me with her positive can-do spirit. She wanted so badly to come to my matches, but she had to work. I honestly don't know if my dad ever came or not; I don't remember seeing him, but he did love the sport, and he was supportive.

Basketball was another story, however. Dad hated the game, which he let me know unequivocally. He didn't tell me I couldn't play, but he did nothing to encourage me either. Clearly I was on my own. I was tall, and therefore a good candidate for the sport. And I was fast, which gave me an advantage over some of the bigger girls, who were just as tall, but not as quick.

Although I was not the greatest dribbler in the world, I could steal the ball quite easily from the opponents, and the coach took notice of me. My good defensive skills and outside shooting got me promoted to the starting line-up, much to the disapproval of the other players. I was one of two rovers, and I was the only white girl on the team. Most of my teammates were from the Lamar Terrace projects, a housing development subsidized by government funding. They looked rough, they talked rough, they were rough. They let me know in graphic detail what they thought of white people, and it wasn't pleasant. The looks I received were enough to make my blood freeze, but I had been down the bully road before, and I wasn't intending to go down it again; when and where to take my stand, however, I did not know.

    The stars on the team were two pugnacious sisters, very dark skinned, and very tall - taller than me. They took their basketball seriously, and cursed me into shape. I befriended them by working hard on the court, and using humor off the court. When I showed them I could hang with them athletically, and wasn't afraid of our differences, I earned their respect, something they did not give out easily. I became their white girl mascot. Not only did they respect my game, they became my guardian angels, and got in the face of the other teammates who tried to take me down. As it turned out, I did not have to take a stand, they took it for me. We had a really good season, and made it to the city championship. My Dad never came to see any of my games.

THE SUITCASE OF SHAME

During my senior year I applied for a private college in Nashville. Dad told me I would never be able to go, he wasn't going to pay for it, and once again, I was on my own. I had good enough grades for a partial scholarship, and by this time my dad had mortgaged our apartment buildings to the hilt, so I was a good candidate for the Basic EducationOpportunity Grant. Mom and I worked tirelessly, filling out the necessary and tedious paperwork, to try to get it in on time. Then it was a matter of crossed fingers and lifted hands in prayer. I believe it was the latter that did the trick. Mom and I celebrated, while Dad pouted. By the end of the summer, however, Dad had gotten used to the idea that I really was leaving Memphis, and leaving him, and he drove me up to school in our white cargo van packed with my belongings. Hidden beneath those belongings, and unbeknownst to me, was a little suitcase marked "shame."

Belmont had its own coteries and cliques, but no bullies. I made it a point to get involved in all activities made available to freshmen. I joined every club, and participated in every event. I was determined not to let the shame from my past, the shame that made me feel "not enough," keep me from becoming everything I could be for the future.

Belmont had a good mix of students. Some were quite well off, some were on scholarships like me, some were off campus students paying their way through school. Many of the students were home grown Baptists, but not every one professed a religion. Quite a few were there for the music program, one of the best in the nation, as it was centered in the heart of Music City. It didn't matter, however, if you were Baptist or Buddhist, chapel attendance was mandatory. For the most part, chapel was boring and everyone either studied or slept, but every once in a while it could be quite entertaining.

One of the more enjoyable chapels was one in which I participated. I had been asked by the Baptist Student Union to write a skit advertising an upcoming event. Not only did I write the skit, I was the skit. My dad had taught me the art of impersonation, and Mae West was just one of many female actresses I could mimic. I wrote the skit around her character, and in Les Ash fashion, dressed the part. Even the music business students woke up and paid attention; the whole audience was in stitches. The crowning point of the skit was when I addressed one of the professors in true Mae West fashion, and begged the question, "Why don't you come up and see me sometime?" Everyone was on the floor, not because of the quote, or even my adorable accent, but because the professor, who I called attention to, was known to be the most prudish man on campus, and the last man in the building to want attention of any kind.

Dr. Modene was also my history professor, and when I arrived late for his class after chapel, he was already in mid lecture position. He looked my way as I entered through the doorway, stopped in mid-sentence, and sputtered, "Oh, my!" He backed up toward his desk, all the while nervously fanning himself with his lecture notes, and clumsily stepped into his wastebasket. This, of course, sent a roar of laughter rippling through the room, into the halls, and into the cafeteria. By the end of the day, everyone on campus had heard the story, and I was called into the Dean's office.

The Dean of women just happened to be Dr. Modene's wife, so I was obviously not going to get much sympathy that afternoon. She was a fine woman with high ideals and morals to match; needless to say, *not* a fan of Mae West. She was aghast that someone of my calibre and Christian upbringing could have pulled such a stunt. I received a forty-five minute lecture on propriety and civility, as well as "lady-like" behavior, with a few scriptures thrown in for good measure. She ended her remonstration with the quote, "It is not the end of the means that matters, but the means to the end." I wasn't quite sure what that meant, but I knew it had something to do with the fact that I had written and performed in a skit that was clearly inappropriate…

and I felt the suitcase of shame open, and spill into the room.

Most of my time at Belmont was filled with great memories, great friends, and great fun. I loved living on campus, playing intramural sports, singing in the musicals, performing in the plays, even loved the classes and all my professors. Life was good away from 1191 Vance, and I blossomed as a person, both within and without. The only other time the suitcase of shame resurfaced while at Belmont was when Vance Street came to visit.

My sophomore year I was in the Belmont Pageant, a preliminary pageant to the Miss Tennessee Pageant. I could not afford a pageant dress like all the other girls, but my mom did her best to make me a lovely pale blue chiffon that I was proud to wear. I had a low sultry voice good for ballads, so I chose a 1940's ballad my dad had introduced to me, during our days of watching black and white movies together. A slinky red satin dress, with a slit down the side, topped off by a black boa, was my costume for the number. Mom made that for me as well.

At rehearsal the band had to modulate the chords to fit my low voice, but they did an excellent job, and I sounded really good. I choreographed the number myself, and made it fun. I used a black Baby Grand as a prop, and started out on top of the piano. I made good use of both the Baby Grand, and the black boa, and the audience loved it. I was more than half way through my number when I saw a door in the back of the auditorium open; I watched as my parents stumbled in the dark to find seats close to the front. My dad was late to every event, so I shouldn't have been surprised. Mom always told him we had to be somewhere an hour early to get him there on time, but that only works for so long.

It took a lot of concentration on my part not to let their abrupt arrival get me off key. I finished strong, and everyone applauded, especially my dad, but I was hurt and disappointed that he only saw the last bit of the performance. It was a big deal for me to be in the pageant. Probably a once-in-a-lifetime experience. I wasn't the most beautiful girl in the group, neither was I the most talented. I wasn't experienced enough to know how to answer the questions in the interview, but one thing I did have going for me was the swimsuit competition. My long legs and flat belly made a nice figure for the one piece I had picked out; but swimsuit only counted for ten percent, and that wasn't going to get me to the top five.

I knew the song I had picked out was not the show stopper the judges were looking for, but I didn't care; because I was excited to have the opportunity to perform, and sing a song that was special to my dad. But my dad didn't care enough to get there on time, and he only heard the ending. After my presentation, as I was waiting backstage during the other performances, I felt a sadness envelop me. I felt like I wasn't good enough to be on Les Ash's priority list. If I had been a horse at the track, he would have been there in time to place the bet; or if I had been his friend Mavie, he would have gotten to the club for the first dance, but once again he had given me his left overs, and the suitcase of shame fell open.

The sadness that had come over me stayed with me until the last beauty took her bow. I stood in line with the other girls as the names of the top five contestants were called; but I paid little attention. My mind had drifted back to Vance Street, and landed somewhere between "less than" and "not enough." I was starting to drift into oblivion when something amazing happened. The Master of Ceremonies called my name. The girl to my right shooed me toward the center of the stage, where last year's winner handed me a beautiful bouquet of long stem roses, hugged me, and congratulated me for winning the title of Miss Congeniality. I was too shocked to know what to say, but did my best to express my gratitude, and walked proudly back to my place in line with trophy in hand. The suitcase of shame closed quietly, and it would not re-open again for a long time…at least not while I was still a student of Belmont College in Nashville, Tennessee.

While at Belmont I tried out for and made the tennis team both freshman and sophomore year. It's where I met my coach, Betty Wise, who was both an inspiration and a friend. Even though I was not the best player on the team, it was her belief in me that gave me the confidence to win; and win I did. My favorite victory was a doubles match at a tournament in Jackson, Tennessee, at a school called Union. The same school my son would attend many years later.

Belmont is also where I made friends for life. It's where I met my best friend, Joanna, whose friendship proved invaluable for the next thirty years. After college, when I returned home, it was Joanna who introduced me to a young dental student named Clay. Clay would become my coach in softball, another sport in which I was quite proficient; and when I became his star player, he took notice. It wasn't long before he called me for a tennis date, and six months later we were married. I had shared a lot of my past with Clay, but I had not shared everything. That would come out in bits and pieces over the course of our marriage.

Clay and I moved to a little Caribbean Island three years after we were married. We were called missionaries, but I never felt comfortable with the title, because, to be quite honest, I never felt like a missionary. I wasn't that holy, not that missionaries are; but the world tries to hold them up as such, and I knew just how ordinary and opposite of that ideal I was. Our firstborn had just turned two when we arrived, and I birthed two more on the island, and one back in the states on a visit. It must be true that you cannot escape your past, because I met a fellow missionary that reminded me of my dad. Needless to say, we sometimes butted heads.

During the Gulf Crisis you could buy plane tickets for a song; the threat of a terrorist attack on planes was being taken seriously, and no one wanted to fly. We told Dad we'd buy his ticket if he wanted to chance it and come see our new baby girl. Mom had already come and gone a few months earlier after the birth of Elizabeth. I was thrilled my dad was willing to take the risk, and I made it my mission to show him a good time.

I took him to Crane beach, one of the more popular tourist spots on the island; it had been the setting for a Chanel No 5 commercial a few years earlier. The hotel had a beautiful rectangular pool adorned with massive Greek columns on one end, and a view to the sea on the other. Both the hotel and pool were built strategically on a ledge that looked down on the frothy blue-green ocean sandwiched between a natural coral reef, and the pure white sand that stretched for miles to both the right and left of the cliff.

The only entrance to the private beach was through the hotel and pool, which led to a steep and narrow set of stone steps descending from the top of the cliff to the beach below. Once my dad and I made it to the bottom of the steps, we began a seaside stroll, looking for beautiful shells to add to the children's collection. The further we walked away from the hotel, the less crowded the beach, until it seemed we were the only ones on the island. In the distance, however, we could see one couple walking toward us.

The closer we got to the couple, the more we could make out the figures, and the figures were rather curvaceous. They belonged to two very attractive women, one with short blonde hair, the other with long brown hair; each having perfect physiques, golden tans, and wearing nothing more than a thong that covered very little of their cheeks. I didn't realize it at the time, but I had brought my dad to a topless beach. When Dad realized he was seeing what he thought he was seeing, he became quite indignant, and began a sermon on the subject of indecency..

"What is this world coming to?" he questioned almost mockingly; his words did not match his tone. I found it both peculiar and humorous that no matter how much my dad disapproved of the women approaching us, he would not take his eyes off of them. I guess he noticed that I noticed.

"I'll show them," he stated emphatically. "I'm not going to let them keep me from enjoying my walk on the beach. I'm just going to stare right at them."

And stare, he did. He looked straight at them (or parts of them) the entire time, from the moment we first noticed the barely visible bosoms until they bounced right passed us. He did not turn his head, he did not blink, he did not speak a word. He showed them all right, and he showed me, too; that even though his morality had kicked in, something else had kicked in as well. He may have been the grandfather to my children, but he was still a man, and he still admired beautiful women.

Dad was a dear the entire week. For five days he was amazing. He helped with the dishes, brought in the laundry, changed the washers in the faucets, and played with the kids. He spent much of the time sprawled out on the floor playing army with the boys, then ticking them incessantly as laughter peeled through the house. He took the older three to the park, and taught them how to hit a baseball. He showed them how to fly the kites he had brought them from back home. He helped them learn the art of floating in the ocean, and how to tell a shark from a dolphin. He carried their tired bodies from the car to the couch, and collapsed in the middle of them as they lay on his lap. He tucked them in at night, then spent an hour sharing stories from his past. After the kids were asleep, he spent the rest of the evening with me on the porch, listening to the ocean rock against the reef while we named the constellations.

My dad was great, and it had been wonderful. On the sixth day of his stay, however, the night before he left for home, he had an episode. I should have seen it coming, but I had enjoyed such a pleasant week, that I let my guard down. We ended the visit poorly; I should have known the normal would not last. It never did.

As I drove my dad to the airport the next morning, the same sick feeling of shame came over me. I regretted we had argued. He had made some unkind remarks, and I had reacted poorly. I was mad at myself for my lack of control, and apologized profusely for my shameful behavior. He apologized as well, and before he boarded the plane we gave each other a long and loving embrace.

As he walked across the tarmac toward the plane that would take him home, I saw him pull his handkerchief from his pant pocket and wipe his eyes. He boarded the plane, and took a seat by the window; he pushed his face against the glass and smiled in my direction. I waved goodbye, and followed him with my eyes as long as I could; the plane turned the corner and started its ascent. I sobbed like a baby all the way home. I was so sad. Sad we had fought. Sad he had left. Sad that I would not see him again for a very long time. But the thing that made me the saddest, was the fact that even though I had grown up, married, had four children, and moved to an island two thousand miles away; I still carried among my belongings the relentless suitcase of shame.

FORGIVENESS

As I lay in my king size bed twenty years after my dad's visit to Barbados, I thought about that suitcase of shame; and the more I read Steven Tracy's book, the more I realized how much that shame had influenced my way of thinking about myself. I also realized that I had carried those feelings with me all through elementary school, junior high, and high school. I had carried that shame with me through four years of college and into marriage. I had even carried it into my parenting and church work. The more I read, the more I became aware that I needed to unload that shame, and before I could do so, I would first have to face the fact that I needed to forgive.

So I searched for the chapter on forgiveness in Tracy's book. When I found it, I saw that it had been well marked with an orange neon highlighter. Apparently another reader needed the chapter on forgiveness as well. Everything I had ever been taught about forgiveness was challenged in this one chapter. I had been taught that if we do not forgive, we will not be forgiven; that even if someone does not seek forgiveness, we must forgive; and that in order to really forgive, we must let go of all negative emotions around the offense, including our memories.

Steven Tracy gave me a much more realistic and helpful understanding of forgiveness. According to him, the act of forgiveness is divided into three parts: judicial forgiveness, psychological forgiveness, and relational forgiveness.(1) I should say at the outset that although Mr. Tracy approaches the act of forgiveness from a biblical perspective, the principles he explains will prove helpful to anyone seeking peace in an unbearable situation. I know they helped me.

According to Tracy, God's desire is to forgive all of humanity in whatever state they are in, and at whatever level of abuse they have perpetrated toward others. This is a forgiveness that knows no bounds, and is a complete removal of all guilt from the guilty. This type of forgiveness removes the sin from the sinner, as far as the east is from the west, never to be recalled again. It can only come from God, and is the reason Christ died on the cross. Churches cannot offer this kind of forgiveness. Individuals cannot offer this kind of forgiveness. Only God, the perfect Judge, can grant this kind of forgiveness, which Tracy calls judicial forgiveness.(2)

Psychological forgiveness consists of both a negative and a positive position: on the downside, you have to practice letting go of hatred, ill feelings, and revenge, while on the upside you strive to extend grace to the one who has hurt you. It doesn't necessarily mean you forget, although with time, depending on the offense, memory loss may and often does occur. But it does mean that in spite of what you will remember, you choose not to exact revenge, not to harbor ill will, not to let hatred eat you alive. You choose to let go.

"Letting go" is not a simple process, however, and takes time. It involves gradual movement toward a different mindset in which negatives are replaced with positives. This is where grace comes in: you practice extending grace through prayer, meditation, and the repeated decision not to dwell on the abuse. As an act of your will, you choose to pray and hope for the perpetrator's healing. And in the end, you are the one who is healed.(3)

Relational forgiveness, the third part, means exactly what it says. It is about restoring the relationship between the victimizer and the victim, the abuser and the abused, the one who hurts, and the one who is hurt. How do you do that? According to Tracy, this forgiveness is always desirable, but not always possible. God's desire for humanity is that the relationship between each person and the Creator be restored, as well as the relationship between persons. However, restoration of a relationship depends on both the abuser and the victim: both parties have to be willing to seek forgiveness and forgive.(4)

It depends on the abuser, insofar as that person must recognize his or her hurtful (and sometimes dangerous) actions, and seek genuine repentance—which by definition means a change in behavior. So, whereas the responsibility for psychological forgiveness lies with the abused, the responsibility for relational forgiveness lies equally with the abused and abuser alike. When we forgive someone psychologically, we remove, from our side, the barriers that hinder relationship; but the perpetrator may still be hiding behind his or her own barrier of denial, avoidance, guilt, or shame. Once the perpetrator acknowledges the hurtful behavior, is truly sorry for it, and seeks forgiveness from his victim, he is on his way to restoring the broken relationship. The real test is whether he cares enough to change his behavior. Tracy gives four indicators of genuine repentance:

1. The abuser takes full responsibility for the abuse (confession);

2. The abuser acknowledges the widespread and extensive damage done to the victim and demonstrates remorse for the harm done;

3. The abuser enacts new boundaries that demonstrate respect for the victim and help ensure that the abuse will not reoccur; and

4. The abuser takes active steps to change the patterns of behavior that led to the abuse.(5)

If the abuser is willing to take these steps, and if the victim has already engaged in psychological forgiveness, then the results are positive. The relationship may never be as wholesome and healthy as before the abuse occurred, but it is certain that with effort by both parties, true restoration can occur and lead to a meaningful reconciliation. There is an old saying, "The deeper the wound, the longer it takes to heal."(6) This is true of any hurtful act. Some relationships will be restored more quickly than others, depending on how deep the wound is.

In the case of my dad and me, we were constantly restoring our relationship. There were a lot of scarred-over wounds, but there were also a lot of beauty marks; for every act of abuse, there had been an act of love. Perhaps that is why I've had a hard time remembering all the episodes of abuse that occurred. Over the years I forgot what most of the altercations were about, but the same feelings were nonetheless quick to resurface whenever my dad had a blow-up. This resurfacing of feelings lasted all my life until my dad's passing. It was important for me to remember what caused the feelings, in order to process their effects on each of us, and try to resolve the pain that was deeply lodged in the innermost recesses of my soul.

Tracy explains it this way: "Facing our brokenness forces us to live in the truth, and helps us to identify and extinguish the destructive lies created by the shame of our abuse... . . . . Facing the shame of past abuse and damage is necessary to mitigate and heal the ongoing effects of trauma. . .... Facing the truth and pain of our past is also necessary in order to experience appropriate, healthy relationships."(7)

I needed to mend my soul, and the only way I could do that was to face my past—to gaze into it, and try to remember both the good and the bad. Then I needed to try to correlate my past experiences with my present pain. While I never blamed my dad for my mistakes, I understood that the way we grow up bears heavily on how we perceive ourselves—and that, consequently, bears heavily on how we react to diverse situations; how we relate to our spouses, children, and others close to us. It probably has an influence on how we relate to everyone.

Some things about my past were significantly beneficial in helping me relate to others. Some were not. Writing the story of growing up with my dad was a way for me to grieve, as well as a way to take a deeper look at what made me tick. Why did I feel the way I did about myself? Why did I react to my husband the way I did? Why did I want so much control over my children? Why did I still have bouts of depression and self-depreciation? What was the reason for my pain? These were the questions I asked myself, questions that screamed for answers.

One day, after more than twenty-five years of marital and parental bliss, life hit me from all sides. I experienced some pretty significant pain, and for a period of five years I probably cried every day—sometimes several times a day. During that time I was dealing with my elderly dad, who was also crying every day. He was remembering his past and longing to be forgiven. His age did not mellow his mood swings, but it certainly made him more vulnerable. He confessed his mistakes to us over and over; and had a deep need to hear us say that we forgave him and loved him, which, of course, we did do and did say.

The reality of my dad's situation was that he was not going to change. All my life I had prayed he would change. I believed he would change after he went to the citywide crusade. I believed he would change after he "walked the aisle" during the spring revival. I believed he would change after he got baptized. I believed he would change after he started attending church. And there were, in fact, some changes: his stand on morality became stronger, and his knowledge that God loved him was dear to him. He certainly knew the Scriptures about wifely submission. He quit smoking, tried not to curse as readily, and voted against the lottery.

But the behavior that had caused the greatest pain did not change. The older he got, the less in control of his emotions and actions he became, and the more prone to mood swings and depression. Forgiveness was an everyday affair, especially for my mother, brother, and sister-in-law. I forgave whenever the occasion called for it.

In looking back upon my growing-up years, however, I realized that a deeper type of forgiveness was called for: not just a forgiveness of the present, but a forgiveness of the past. If my past had such an enormous influence on my present, then I wanted to analyze it as critically and honestly as possible, to understand all the nuances involved in my evolution as a person, to accept the good and forgive the bad. To do that I decided to take a look at my dad's life, as well as my own. I wanted to break it down, lift out every piece of data, and use the information to mend my soul. I knew the process would be uncomfortable, and at times even painful, but it might also bring to light why my dad did what he did, and why I did what I did. I wanted to figure things out. I wanted to understand.

THE BLOW-UPS

Why did my dad have so many blow-ups? Everyone gets angry at times, some more than others; but my dad routinely had blow-ups that he seemed unable to control. When I was growing up, we never talked about the mental condition called bipolar disorder; we did not know it existed. We just thought Dad blew up because things didn't go his way. We just thought he had an anger management issue. Or worse, we thought we did something to cause his ranting.

When my dad was in his seventies, my mom and brother wanted him to go to the doctor to get some much-needed help. Steve took a thirty-seven-page handwritten letter, my dad had composed several years earlier, and gave it to the doctor to read. Recently, Mom found the letter and showed it to me. It had been written with us (his family) in mind; I had read it over thirty years ago, but had long since forgotten it. When I reread it, I was reminded of the sadness I constantly felt for my dad. The following is an excerpt:

> "You would think I would have learned my lesson by this time. But not ole Les. He's hard-headed and stubborn. He has to learn at

the old school of "hard knocks," and still he keeps coming back for more. But you know, I'm not as young as I once was, and I'm not as strong as I once was—not physically—not mentally. I'm afraid I can't take it like I once could, and spring back. Years of constant failure takes something out of you, and you begin to wonder, "What's the use?" Why continue to beat your head against a brick wall? Well, that's the point I'm at now, and I'm tired of trying to fight fate and constantly coming up the loser. I no longer have what it takes to keep going against what seem to be insurmountable odds. I'm finished; I'm through; I'm all washed up; I'm kaput."

Dad wrote this after another failed business venture. He went on to say that if we had just helped him more, he would have succeeded. He finished by blaming us for his failures, and suggested we look into a mirror and examine ourselves.

The doctor read the letter, along with all the other notes my brother and mom had compiled describing my dad's actions; then diagnosed my dad with bipolar disorder. By this time, we had already figured that out, but it was helpful to have the confirmation. The doctor prescribed Lithobid for

Dad, and when he took it, Mom was delighted with the new and improved Les: he was calm, easy-going, and less demanding. But he was also lethargic. Dad hated the new Les. He said being on the medication made him feel strange, as if someone else were controlling him. It made him feel different from others, and the stigma associated with a disorder of any kind was offensive to him. He did not want to believe he had a problem. He stayed on the medication less than a month, and then stopped taking the pills. Mom tried to sneak them into his food and drink, but Dad was too alert to let that happen. Eventually Mom gave up, and the old Les resurfaced.

After Dad died I wanted to understand a bit more about bipolar disorder. I figured that if I understood Dad's disease, I might understand why he had done the things he did. I wasn't interested in teaching a course on the subject; I just wanted to understand it from a layman's point of view. I wanted a book I could easily digest, one that would give me answers I could comprehend without needing a doctorate in psychology to interpret them.

I found such a book: *Overcoming Bipolar Disorder*, by Mark Bauer and several other doctors and nurses, including some with doctorates in psychiatry, mental health disorders, biology, and epidemiology. It is a comprehensive workbook for understanding and managing bipolar disorder. It was interesting to me that the authors of this book agreed with other care providers and scientists that bipolar disorder is a "complex combination of biological, psychological, and social factors" referred to as bio-psychosocial illness. Although not a doctor myself, or even a student of mental disorders, after over fifty years of living with my dad, I could have told the authors this was true. My dad's persona was the combined result of a chemical imbalance (biological), the environment he grew up in (social), and the way he viewed himself (psychological).(8)

I wanted to understand more about the meaning of a chemical imbalance, so I read up on the subject. The clearest definition I found came from The Neurogistics Brain Wellness Program created by expert clinicians to aid in the balance and well-being of the brain. They explained that chemicals called neurotransmitters, stored in the nerve cells in the brain, provide the mechanism by which individual neurons communicate with one another.

These chemicals are norepinephrine, epinephrine, serotonin, GABA, and dopamine, and they are used in the brain either to stimulate or to inhibit. Norepinephrine and epinephrine are excitatory neurotransmitters that can affect mood swings, sleep cycles, and the ability to focus; serotonin and GABA are inhibitory neurotransmitters that help to stabilize mood, and balance the over-firing of excitatory neurotransmitters. If these two sets of chemicals are out of balance, the person's emotional highs and lows will be as well. The remaining chemical, dopamine, can be either excitatory or inhibitory. Imbalances of dopamine can contribute to depression, lack of focus, lack of motivation, inability to stay on task, and forgetfulness.(9)

These imbalances were evident in my dad from the very beginning of his adult life. I remember his emotional highs and lows, his forgetfulness, his inability to stay on task, irregular sleep cycles, and severe depression. Whether or not these neurotransmitters were the reason for his temper, I do not know. He definitely had an anger problem, and the imbalance of emotions could have been a contributing factor; but I tend to think his environment and upbringing may have played a more dominant role in that aspect of his character.

Dad was very close to his mother, Bernice. She was a self-made woman who pretty much pulled herself up by her bootstraps in order to make a living for herself and my dad. She was married three times; the first and last time were to the same man, Edward Wilson, my father's father. My grandmother was not a beauty, but she was attractive in her own way. She was good-natured, and although not educated past the third grade, very savvy. She was a hard worker who knew how to take a dollar and turn it into ten. This may have been the attraction for Edward, who was not one to keep a job very long; he used his good looks to get what he wanted, which was mostly alcohol and women. He never contributed much to the household, apart from a stern voice, an iron hand, and a negative role model for a young boy.

After Bernice divorced Edward she married an entirely different type of man. Whereas Edward had been a macho ladies man, Dad Shumaker was more like a little boy. He came from wealthy parents who disapproved of Bernice and her son. In fact, they cut him out of their will, and took away all access to the family money, because he had married beneath him and them. Dad Shumaker made the barest of livings by running reels at a local movie theater, so Grandma had to be the main player in providing for their home.

After Dad Shumaker was killed by a drunk driver, Bernice pulled herself up again, and made a very good living by buying property, and converting it into family dwellings which she rented out. By the time Edward came back into her life, she had a little nest egg saved up, and was doing quite well financially. Edward saw her good fortune, and being the opportunist he was, decided he wanted a piece of the pie. He sweet-talked Grandma into marrying him again, but the situation was different now: Les had grown up, found a beautiful wife, and they had a son.

Edward thought he could manage that. He knew he had a good thing going: a roof over his head, food on the table, and freedom to do whatever he wanted. What he didn't realize was that he no longer had the hold on Grandma he'd once enjoyed; he'd been replaced, and a new king sat on the throne. King Steven was the apple of Grandma's eye, and when Edward started correcting him in the same stern, heavy-handed way he had once used on my dad, Grandma sent him packing. Edward left willingly when he realized she wasn't going to turn over her assets to the man who had already walked out on her once before.

When I think about my dad's upbringing, I have to imagine the pain he felt as a little boy, whose only interaction with his dad was negative. His dad was a poor provider who constantly drank, had a child by another woman, and was not around much. When he was around, he was unrelentingly harsh. Dad's stepdad had provided some comic relief with his pranks and antics, but again, had been a poor role model for success or provision.

Dad had no one to show him the way except his hard-working mother, who was too tired after working all day to pay much attention to his emotional needs or behavior. At a very young age Dad was left most of the day to fend for himself, and ended up getting into quite a bit of mischief. This led to more bad behavior, which had the makings of out-and-out rebellion. Dad was just enough of a rebel to want to experience life his way - without convention, ground rules, or discipline.

This ungrounded, undisciplined, young man spent the next twenty years trying to make something out of himself in a world where convention, rules, and discipline are necessary commodities. As his failures increased, so did his low self-esteem: with each setback, he further doubted his ability and his future. These were the seeds planted in his mind and soul, and fed by the chemical mayhem in his body, they sprouted into the bipolar disorder he came to refer to as his "demon."

How did the "demon" affect us? To answer that question best, I decided to read more about it from a clinician's point of view. As I read about the disorder, I felt a knot twist in my stomach, because what I read was very much in sync with what I had experienced and witnessed during my growing-up years. The first thing that jolted me was the Bipolar Spectrum Diagnostic Scale in the *Overcoming Bipolar Disorder* workbook. I checked off almost every description listed. The following is a list of traits Dad exhibited during his manic/depressive episodes:

- Mood levels shift drastically from time to time and change like a switch.

- Mood/energy level can be very low, and at other times very high.

- During the low periods they tend to stay in bed a lot.

- The individual has no motivation to do the things they need to do.

- They often feel blue, sad all the time, depressed, and hopeless.

- Their ability to function at work or socially is impaired.
- Typically the low phases last for a few weeks, but can last just a few days.
- Individuals will have periods in between these low phases where they feel normal.
- The energy then increases and they get much accomplished and feel a high.
- During these high periods they may feel irritable, on edge, or aggressive, even hyper.
- During these high periods, they take on too many activities at once.
- They spend money in ways that will get them into trouble.
- They are more talkative, outgoing, and sexual during high periods.
- They may get into difficulty with co-workers and police or others in authority.(10)

When Dad was high, he was a man on a mission. This is when he started his new businesses, invested in moneymaking ventures, gambled at the track, constructed a three-story Christmas tree, built a homemade trailer, and danced the jitterbug all night. When he was low he kicked over scrambled eggs, threw plates on the floor, put his foot through the television, punched his fist through the wall, packed a suitcase, packed a pistol, stomped out of the house, or slept for two weeks.

When he was high, music played constantly throughout the house. When he was low, the sounds of snoring were the only notes I heard. When he was high, the grass was green and the sky was blue. When he was low, the grass was always greener on the other side, and he was blue. When he was high, he smelled of Old Spice aftershave on a clean, smooth face. When he was low, he just smelled. When he was high, we danced and laughed. When he was low, we walked on eggshells and kept quiet. When he was high, all was right with the world, and God was in his heaven. When he was low, nothing was right, and Les was in his hell.

According to the authors of *Overcoming Bipolar Disorder*, irritability and anger can raise their ugly head in either the low or high period. "Everyone experiences feelings of anger or irritability, but people with bipolar disorder are especially prone to these feelings and the adverse effects of anger. In fact, sudden feelings of anger or irritability are key symptoms of mania… However, anger and irritability can also be part of depression, and sometimes the most prominent aspect of depression, at least as experienced by the people around someone with bipolar disorder."(11)

It's hard for me to remember whether Dad's blow-ups occurred mainly in his manic state, or in his depressive state; it was probably a little of both. I think he may have become agitated and overly aggressive when he was manic, because he was pumped up, wanting to accomplish much, and things did not go according to plan. However, I think his biggest blow-ups came in his depressed state, when he experienced the greatest defeats.

An example of this is the time he started the small gift shop out east. He used up all his capital purchasing merchandise for the store, and needed more to keep the business afloat. Unable to get it from the bank, he went to Grandma Bernice. When she refused to lend him more money, he got angry, but the anger found expression around other things; leaving the cap off the toothpaste, or not refilling the water jug in the refrigerator. He wasn't really angry about the toothpaste; anger had built up inside him because he was discouraged about the way the business was going. After he ranted and raved over insignificant things for a few days, he would fall into a depressed state. This was when he developed negative thought patterns, and believed everyone was against him, a feeling that haunted him all his life.

When going through Dad's files after his death, Mom found several more handwritten letters on yellow stained notebook paper...one written shortly before he passed. The letters were filled with accusations that we were all against him, that *everyone* was against him. These letters were a stained glass window into his soul—a window splattered with paranoia and despair. On the bright side, however, she also found some lovely letters that told of the love he felt for his family, how proud of us he was, and how lucky he believed he was to have the family he had. These letters reflected the cycle of emotions he experienced constantly.

Dad's cycles usually began with mania. He got on a high and formulated a plan; then something went wrong with the plan, and he needed money to fix it; he couldn't get the money, so he couldn't fix the plan; he became frustrated and angry so he blew up; he apologized; he gave up and became depressed; he thought the whole world was against him; he slept it off; he woke up in a more or less normal state, and was happy for about a week; he got restless; something piqued his interest and his mood improved; he formulated another plan; and the cycle began again.

It is my belief, based on stories I heard all my life, that this pattern was in place for years before I was even in the picture. I didn't understand the pattern as a young girl; I just knew that something was wrong. I felt sorry for my dad, but at the same time I feared his anger. I now know that Dad's anger was his way of releasing and expressing deep-seated feelings lodged in his heart and mind ever since he was a young boy. According to the authors of *Overcoming Bipolar Disorder*,

> Anyone's past life history can contribute to the way they react or overreact to situations. For instance, people who have been ridiculed, neglected, or victimized in the past may have built up negative feelings over time based on these events. Sometimes it is not the person or the event in the present that makes you feel angry, but it's your way of thinking—based on your past personal experiences—that creates these angry feelings.(12)

This was true not only of my dad, but of my brother and me as well.

MY BROTHER AND ME

Although six years apart in age, my brother and I were very close. We never fought or argued; Steve looked out for me, took care of me, and was always there for me. He filled the gap left void by Dad's manic depressive cycles. He never saw me as a tag-a-long. Instead, he made sure to arrange his schedule to include me; like the time he fixed a seat for me on the back of his bike and took me to his baseball practice; or when he tried to teach me to play the guitar so I could "be" in his band. But my favorite memory is when he gave me the confidence to do something that felt impossible. I don't remember what Dad was into during that season of my life, but he wasn't the one to teach me how to ride a bike…it was my brother.

My bike was a hand-me-down and a little too big for me to manage, so there were training wheels attached. I wanted so badly to be able to ride with the big kids, to ride a bike without aids, like my friends. I had tried several times without the training wheels, only to fall and skin my knees, making me bike-shy and scared to try again. My brother watched as I worked hard to keep up with the neighborhood kids, but their bikes could move quite a bit faster, being unencumbered by an additional sets of wobbly helpers. One Saturday morning Steve had seen enough and said it was time I put away my childish ways.

He escorted me and my bike up the street to a doctor's office that sat in front of a vacant parking lot.

"Okay, Audrey, I am going to take off your training wheels, and I want you to get on your bike and ride without them."

"I'll try," I shrugged my shoulders resignedly.

So I got on my bike and peddled about three feet before the bike started weaving from one side to the other, and eventually fell to the ground trapping my right leg under its frame. When I looked at my leg and saw a small amount of blood oozing from where the chain had scraped my calf, I started crying…more from the disappointment than from the pain.

"You okay, Audrey?" my brother rushed to my aide.

"I guess, but I want to go home."

"You can't quit now. You made it three feet. Next time you will go even further." he encouraged.

"I'll never be able to do it," I protested. "I can't ride a bike."

"Yes, you can. You just need a little confi…" stopping in mid sentence.

"I need what?" giving him a quizzical look.

"You know what you need?" he asked perkily. You need my magic key!"

"What magic key?"

"When I was your age, Dad gave me a magic key to help me ride my bike. As long as I had the magic key I could not fall."

"Really?" I was encouraged.

"Sure!" he spoke with conviction. "Here," he reached into his pocket and pulled out one single metallic key and placed it in my hand. "All you have to do is hold on to this key while you ride your bike, and you won't fall off."

"Wow!" I believed in Santa Clause. It wasn't hard to believe in a magic key if my brother said so.

So I clutched the key in my palm as I squeezed the handle bars, and hopped back on the bike my brother was steadying for me. Steve let go of the bike, gave me a little push, and sent me rolling down the slanted asphalt. My bike did not weave one bit, and as I turned the corner around the doctor's office I looked at my brother and smiled. I was doing it! I was actually doing it! As I circled back around from the other side of the building I headed straight for my brother who was cheering me on. I stopped on a dime in front of him, and he reached out to grab the bike bars again.

"Good job, Audrey! I knew you could do it!" Steve exclaimed proudly.

When we got back home my brother took the key back. When he returned it to me it was on a piece of ribbon that I could loop around my neck, making it easier to keep up with when riding. For the next several weeks I made sure I had the magic key necklace when I mounted my bike; I could finally ride as fast as my friends.

One Saturday Steve took the key away from me again, and told me I had to ride my bike without it. I got mad at him and told him he was crazy. I wasn't going to ride my bike without the magic key. He told me the magic from the key had been transferred to me, and I no longer needed to have the key around my neck for the magic to work. He took me outside and stayed with me until I tried riding my bike without the key. Much to my surprise, I did great; I did not fall once.

After Steve saw that I was able to ride without any problems, he proceeded to tell me the truth. Dad had never given him a key, and there was no such thing as magic. He had just given me the key to give me confidence. He said since I didn't believe in myself, he gave me something I could believe in. He told me I did an amazing job; but in my heart, I knew who the amazing one was that day. My brother had stepped in when my dad was preoccupied, and taught me how to ride my first real bike. The key may not have been magical, but the relationship between my brother and me was.

Those were sweeter times; we were still young and not yet tainted. As we got older the experiences of our home life affected us in ways that were darker; and the environment that my brother and I grew up in contributed to the way we reacted and overreacted to many situations. I saw this never more clearly in my brother than one night when we were all eating at a restaurant, and he almost got into a knife fight with a couple of men close by. We were all adults by this time, and had gone out to celebrate my mom's birthday. The party next to our table had been drinking quite a bit, and their language was getting out of hand, so Dad took action. He could match the worst offender with his own four-letter words, but he rarely cursed in public, and only when he was provoked; he had a great disdain for men who "cursed like sailors" in front of women and children.

Dad leaned over to their table and politely asked the men to watch their language since there were ladies present. The men did not take well to my dad's chastisement and threatened him; but before my dad could respond, Steve stood up and shoved his face into theirs with his own threats. His anger rose faster than anything I had ever seen in my dad; and he told the men in no uncertain terms, with language I had never heard him use before, that if they tried anything with my dad, he would send them bleeding to the floor before they knew what hit them. For a few minutes I feared my brother even more than I feared my dad—not for me, but for himself. I feared what he might do, and how it would end up.

Steve was out of control. His reaction was a result of pent-up hostility that he had both witnessed and experienced himself for twenty years. Ironically, the man who had dished it out to my brother for decades was the very man he was defending. Thankfully, Dad was neither manic nor depressed that night, and talked my brother down. The men at the adjacent table had enough sense to keep quiet the rest of the evening, and a possible fiasco, as well as a night in jail were averted.

I saw my own pent-up hostility come to surface once I married and had children. I reacted in ways other than anger. Among other things, I exaggerated the evils of alcohol and had a hard time understanding that drinking with restraint was not only acceptable, but part of the multi-faceted culture described in the biblical narrative. My judgmental attitude was highly offensive to one of my sons, and not understood by the other. It took several years before I finally reached the point that I could let go of the anxiety I felt in the presence of social drinking.

And when one of my daughters started dating someone whose religious beliefs did not match my own, I overreacted and handled the entire situation poorly, which put a huge wedge between the two of us. When it came to my female children I had a stubborn pride that caused havoc in our mother/daughter relationships. Being the mom, I should have taken the lead by steering our relationships with wisdom and understanding; but it took years for me to recognize the error of my controlling ways. I am still working on regaining the trust I lost through the inept handling of my sweet girls.

I know my upbringing, family dynamics, and how I viewed myself played a huge role in how I responded to my kids. I allowed my personal fears and regrets to influence the way I dealt with situations, and made a lot of mistakes, especially as a parent of adult children. This fact caused me a great deal of pain, which was part of the five-year depression I experienced. Going through that depression, however, changed me and my perspective. It changed my way of thinking about my family, and about myself.

There was something else that played an important part in the changes that took place in me, and that was my husband's new-found faith. At first I hated him for it. The very core of our marriage had been based on the fact that we were in sync when it came to our beliefs about God. It was one of the things that had attracted me the most, and the thing that had held us together through every season of our life. It was the center of our world, the one area I knew I could always count on. When he changed that core, it was like he had pulled a rug out from under me. More than a rug—more like the earth itself, and I was falling into oblivion.

When he totally changed his belief system, the one I had been brought up to trust as certain truth all my life, it rocked my world. Eventually I grew in my understanding of my husband's new faith, but for five years I struggled more profoundly than I have words to describe. At the time of my dad's death, I was still struggling with this change in my husband, and it made me angry—very, very angry.

I felt so out of control. The anger I carried was buried under a mask I wore to the outside world, but it was real to me. I don't think even my husband understood the torment I was feeling. I was so unhappy. I remember thinking that this was not what I had signed on for.. I felt stuck in a situation I had no control over, and for which I had no answer. I was on a lifeboat trying to survive, and I didn't know how long I could last. What with the passing of my dad during this time, so much was going on within me, that I did not know who or what was the cause of my distress. At any rate, the reading I did to try to understand my dad's, helped me take a deeper look at my own. It helped me see where anger originates, and how it builds.

As outlined clearly in *Overcoming Bipolar Disorder*, anger is caused by stress, life events, frustration, fear, resentment, and disappointment. We can experience stress when faced with problems relating to health, money, work, or personal concerns. When we remember bad things that have happened to us, we can get angry. We can be frustrated by a lack of control over a situation or by a task that overwhelms us. Resentment happens when we feel hurt, rejection, or oppression. When expectations are not met, we feel disappointed.(13)

This described my dad perfectly. These were the triggers that caused his anger. I know he hated the blow-ups as much as we did; I don't know if he could help himself. At the time I thought he could, and his failure to do so caused deep resentment on my part. After much reading and reflection, however, I wonder if it was more outside his control than I realized. I understand that people with this disorder can live full and meaningful lives, but they have to recognize what is going on and get help. They have to learn how to manage their lives, and take steps to minimize the highs and lows.

But this also described me. My anger was a result of all of the above. I felt stressed over the health, money, work, and personal problems facing almost every one of my children. I felt frustrated that I had no control over any of it, nor could I help. I felt frustrated that I had no control over some of the choices my husband had made that caused me grief. I felt fear that I was losing every relationship dear to me. I felt resentment toward both Clay and the kids when they slighted, rejected, or ignored me. I realize now I was looking through a self-absorbed lens, and they probably had the same resentment toward me; but at the time it seemed that nothing had turned out the way I had hoped or expected.

To be honest, my expectations had been too high. They did not reckon with real people in a real world. They did not account for the pain that can be inflicted by accident, by others, or by our own choices. My expectations also did not account for the possibility that a more difficult path may produce a better outcome. I had raised my kids with a kind of proverbial faith that if I just did everything I could to bring them up right, they would make perfect choices, and have a perfect life. When things did not end up as planned, I blamed myself for not doing a good enough job. Not only was this a self-righteous condemnation of my own children, but it was a wrong way to think about myself. It took years for me to change these judgmental thought patterns.

My oldest son fell in love with a beautiful young divorcee. Not only was she a wonderful woman, but she appeared to be a perfect match for Michael; the one who could keep him on a good path. I was happy that he had found someone so lovely both inside and out after waiting patiently for a very long time. I had been raised in a conservative religious circle where divorcees were treated a little like second class citizens. I did not agree with this theological view; my own brother had been divorced and remarried, but I did understand the idea of potential challenges associated with the baggage of ex-spouses.

I expressed some realistic concerns to my son, which led him to believe that I disapproved of his new wife (which I did not). It would take much work on my part to prove to both of them just how much I did appreciate and approve of their union. Over that time I learned some hard lessons, and the pain involved in the process only added to my depressed state. But I kept trying, and kept eating a steady diet of crow.

When my second son married a girl from out west and moved to a place eighteen hours away, I was sad again. I kept this to myself because I didn't want my personal emptiness to take away from their excitement. They were ideally suited and very much in love, so of course I was happy for them; but it was hard knowing I would only see them once or twice a year. I suppose I could have handled the distance better had I been closer to my other children, but sadly, I was far from all of them both geographically and relationally.

I felt like an outsider in my own home; an orphaned child standing in the cold, looking through a window into a cozy room full of happy people enjoying Christmas dinner without me. I went to church every Sunday with a smile on my face, and when I cried during the song service, people just thought I was an emotional worshiper. I cried every day—at church, at home, in the car, in my bed. I routinely cried myself to sleep, waking up later in the middle of the night, and going into the living room to cry some more. I wasn't sleeping or eating well. I felt like I had bipolar disorder myself—and maybe I did: maybe it ran in the family.

I got out the book and began reading again, hoping to find some help. The authors offered practical advice about how a person with bipolar disorder could reduce the anger and depression. Sleep is important, they said; eating right is important, and physical exercise and hobbies are important. Meeting regularly with a professional who has expertise about the disorder is helpful. Meeting with a counselor to help address unresolved emotions from past experiences is almost a necessity, and family therapy can also be helpful. It's important to enlarge your social circles to include friends who really care about you and your family, and to become involved in your community or church. And above all, it is necessary to treat the disorder as a medical issue and get the proper medication.

Had someone understood what was happening to my dad back then, and had we gotten some help early on, things would have been different for all of us, not only as children but as adults. Had we known to get medication for him, or counseling for the rest of us, then perhaps our lives might have been normal, or at the very least more peaceful. That was not the case, however, and the rest is history.

CODEPENDENCY

"A codependent person is one who has let another person's behavior affect him or her, and who is obsessed with controlling that person's behavior."(14)

One evening while visiting my brother, I overheard him and his wife talking about how my mom was codependent on my dad. I had never really thought about their relationship in this way; but after reading Melody Beattie's book *Codependent No More*, I realized that not only was my mother codependent, but so were the rest of us who had lived with my dad. We all exhibited traits of at least some degree of codependency.

I could even trace this codependency back to my grandmother. Mom had pleaded with Dad for them to move out of my grandmother's house, and start a home of their own. She believed that if Dad could be encouraged to make it on his own, without the luxury of knowing he could fall back on his mom, things could be different for them as a couple. He would have been forced to work at working, and in the process, would have gained self-respect from his own accomplishments and success as a provider—something he very much wanted all his life but never achieved.

After much encouragement from my mom, my dad did go to Grandma, and told her they were going to move out. Grandma pleaded with him not to go, arguing that he would be unable to make it on his own. She contended that he needed to stay with her until he could support his family with a more lucrative job. No doubt she thought she was doing the loving thing, but history proved it was probably the worst thing she could have done for Dad. As it happened, he and my mom never did move out, and we lived with my grandmother until the day she died.

My grandmother was codependent on my dad, and had been since he was born. He was the one constant male figure in her checkered existence. Her first husband had been a disappointment, and her second husband was deceased. Dad was her solace and her purpose; she couldn't bear the thought of being without him. She was dependent on him for emotional support, and didn't realize that she had set him up for failure by insisting he fill that need. I am not blaming her, only recognizing that her codependency and loneliness blinded her to what was right for my dad and his future family.

Melody Beattie describes my grandmother well in this expanded definition of codependency: "But the heart of the definition and recovery lies not in the other person—no matter how much we believe it does. It lies in ourselves, in the ways we have let other people's behavior affect us and in the ways we try to affect them: the obsessing, the controlling, the obsessive "helping," care-taking... peculiar dependency on peculiar people, attraction to and tolerance for the bizarre, other-centeredness that results in abandonment of self, communication problems, intimacy problems, and an ongoing whirlwind trip through the five-stage grief process."(15)

Grandma did the best she could. She was a woman of her time and of her circumstances. I am very proud of her. She was a good friend to my mom, and a wonderful grandmother to my brother and me. Despite a hard and disappointing life in many respects, she was a positive, hardworking woman of faith, and a remarkable person. Everyone loved and respected her; we did too. But it is significant that whenever there was a fork in the road for my mom and dad, Grandma exerted an undue influence on the direction they took. My dad could and should have told her he was moving out. He could have stood his ground, and told her he felt it was the right thing for his family. Instead, he chose the easy way, which left my mom crying for days. I think it was because he was codependent on Grandma as well.

Codependency takes all forms. It can manifest as sheltering, protecting, submitting, rescuing, controlling, reacting, attaching, enabling, and care-taking. Daughters can become mothers; mothers can become wives. Sons can become fathers, and wives can become daughters. Such was the case in our family: my grandmother played the role of both mother and wife to my dad, while my mom submitted to the role of daughter. My dad played the role of both husband and son to my grandmother. It was a dysfunctional triangle which led to a dysfunctional family.

After my grandmother died, the dynamics changed again. My mom added caretaker to her role, assuming Grandma's place in providing for our family. However, no matter how much my mom contributed in this area, Dad still treated her as subservient, and she continued to submit. This went on for years, even after Steve had left the scene to marry. I spent my summers at home while in college, often taking on the role of mother myself, especially when it came time to sell our apartments. Eventually, somewhere along the line, my brother and I took on the role of parents for both our mom and dad, making sure they had a house to live in, and a car to drive.

This came with a price for all of us. We could not give Dad the respect he so desired, because we resented having to take care of him. We tended to pity him, and felt compelled to solve his problems or offer unwanted advice; to take control, or to say yes when we wanted to say no. We felt angry that we had to do for him what he should have been doing for us. When our "little boy" suffered disappointment, we felt sad and picked up the pieces for him in the aftermath of blow-ups. We felt victimized and bitter because what we did for him was not appreciated, while at the same time feeling guilty that we never did enough.

Through all of this we felt different from other families, ashamed of our family, and isolating ourselves socially from peer groups. Most of all, we felt abused.

I hate to even use the word "abuse" because it has such a contemptible connotation, but the truth is that my dad was very abusive. I know his bipolar condition was the cause of his anger and depression, but there was no excuse for the verbal abuse and manipulation he subjected us to—especially my mom, who used her whole existence to serve our family's needs, particularly Dad's.

According to Steven Tracy, "Verbal abuse is a form of emotional maltreatment in which words are systematically used to belittle, undermine, scapegoat, or maliciously manipulate another person. Verbal abuse can be every bit as damaging as physical or sexual abuse, and in some cases it's even more damaging. Those who haven't experienced abuse often can't understand this. The somewhat subjective nature of verbal abuse can make it more insidious and difficult to confront (which can also make it more damaging)."(16)

Dad never understood that the way he talked to Mom was abusive. I remember speaking to him about it one afternoon. He had been in a great mood, very happy, very positive about life, and talking to me in a way that made me feel like our relationship merited a deeper conversation. In fact, I felt so comfortable with him that I thought I could be honest with him. I was wrong. My first mistake was telling him how much I liked seeing him "this way."

"What way?" he asked.

"You know, all positive and happy," I answered.

"I am always positive," he exclaimed defensively. "I am the most positive person on the planet!"

"Well, sometimes you say things that are kind of negative...and a little abusive," I mustered the nerve to explain.

"Don't tell me I am abusive! You don't even know the meaning of the word. I have never been abusive! You are just a young girl, and you are talking to your father," his voice getting stronger and louder with each word. "Have I ever hurt you in any way? Ever hit you?"

"No," I stuttered as I backed away.

"Then don't say I am abusive!" he exploded. "People can get in a lot of trouble for that. There are men out there who have gone to jail unjustly because some woman screamed abuse. It's your mother and your grandmother that are the negatives ones. They are the ones you should be talking to...not me!"

"Yes sir," I muttered sheepishly.

"Now go to your room," he commanded.

I was a grown college woman, but I went to my room; I never used the word abuse again…not to his face.

Truth is, he didn't have a clue. He had no idea how he sounded when he spoke to us, nor did he remember the horrible things he said. There were many times I wanted to record him, because he always denied his temper and his words, claiming he had said, "nothing of the sort." The abuse wasn't always loud and angry. Sometimes the abuse had a more subtle and condescending tone; the way a master talks to a slave who he is trying to keep in place. My dad actually did think he was the master of our home; and although he loved my mom, he talked down to her like the overlord he thought he was.

As sovereign of our household, he did expect things to be done a certain way, and when carried out to his specification, he was the first to applaud; but he expressed his displeasure more often than not, especially to our mom. She didn't discipline the kids enough. She didn't prepare the food well. She didn't iron his shirts correctly. She was not proficient in folding his laundry. Her hair was too short. Her dress was too long. Her weight was too much. Her support was too little.

His biggest complaint was that she didn't understand him. She didn't want to have fun with him. She wasn't willing to go out and dance with him all night. (He didn't recognize the reality of the situation; while he had been enjoying a leisurely day at the house, and had ample energy for foot stomping, she, on the other hand, had been working all day at the office, and just wanted to put her feet up.) She wasn't loving enough, whatever that meant. Actually, I was pretty sure I knew what that meant. Dad didn't understand that a man cannot belittle a woman all day, and then expect her to meet his needs at night. Women don't work that way. They cannot turn on a dime the way a man can. Making her feel like she was the problem in their sex life was pretty demeaning, but the worst abuse came when he wanted money.

Mom was the one paying the bills, the insurance, and the mortgage. She bought the groceries, paid the utilities, and put gas in the car. She didn't have a lot of surplus money to hand over, but Dad thought she should be able to secure a loan anytime he wanted extra cash. He knew how to wear her down, and would use all kinds of tactics to do so. He would start with reason; she needed to see the big picture. If that didn't work, he would beg; and when that didn't work, he would use guilt, accusing her of holding him back. To add insult to injury, he would tell her he would have been a success had it not been for her. If this type of manipulation didn't work, he would launch into an angry tirade, assaulting her with his tongue. The hurtful words did the trick, and Mom handed over not only the money, but her self-esteem.

This sequence was pretty much routine. After every episode, Mom would express to me that she must be the problem. "Maybe if he had married someone else, he would have been a success." If I heard that once, I heard it a hundred times. She really thought, had been made to think, that much of his failure was because of her. She let what he said about her become how she saw herself, even though none of the things he said were true.

She never had the money or means to take care of just herself—not that she particularly needed to, as she was a natural beauty. We all came first, and any extra money was spent on us. She gave us her money, her time, her energy, and her talents; but the one thing she did not give us was her thoughts. I never really knew how she felt about the abuse, because she never opened up to us. She just took it, excused it, echoed Dad's negative comments about herself, and tried her best to please. She constantly defended Dad, bragged on him, and encouraged him. She met his every need from sunup to sundown. If she spent all day typing for her boss, she spent all evening typing for her master. Not one thing did he ask that she didn't try to do for him. She did express on occasion that she needed a break, but if she took that break, it wasn't long before she wanted to get back to him. Mom was codependent.

Melody Beattie believes that codependents think and feel responsible for other people—for their feelings, thoughts, actions, choices, wants, needs, well-being or lack thereof, and ultimate destiny. Codependents may feel anxiety, pity, and guilt when other people have a problem. They may find themselves saying yes when they mean no, doing things they don't really want to do, doing more than their fair share of the work, and doing things other people are capable of doing for themselves. They may not know what they want and need; or if they do, they tell themselves it is not important.

Codependents may abandon their own routine in order to respond to or do something for somebody else. They may feel guilty about spending money or time on themselves. They may blame themselves for everything, think they're not quite good enough, and push their thoughts and feelings aside because of fear and guilt. They may stay busy so they don't have to think about things.

Codependents may feel controlled by other people's anger. They may stay loyal to their compulsions and to the people they believe need them, even to their own detriment. Codependents may not seek help, because they think the problem isn't bad enough or that they aren't important enough.(17)

My brother and I were codependent on my dad as well. Some professionals say that codependency isn't a disease, but a normal reaction to abnormal people.(18) Webster's definition of abnormal is "opposite of normal"; the definition of normal is "usual or average."(19) Other synonyms for normal are ordinary, run of the mill, typical, routine, orderly, right-minded, rational, sound, healthy, reasonable, common, and mentally balanced.(20)

Steve and I were normal, but if the definition and synonyms listed above hold true, then we were living in an abnormal situation with an abnormal father. Les was certainly not ordinary or run of the mill. He was not the typical dad with the typical routine. Did he have days when he was right-minded, sound, reasonable, and rational? Absolutely! Did he have days when he was not? Definitely! Steve and I grew up adoring the reasonable and rational dad, and rescuing the abnormal one.

Melody Beattie explains it this way: "Rescuing and Caretaking mean almost what they sound like. We rescue people from their responsibilities. We take care of people's responsibilities for them. Later we get mad at them for what they've done. Then we feel used and sorry for ourselves. This is the pattern."(21) Elaborating, she continues:

> We become resentful and angry at the person we have so generously 'helped.' We've done something we didn't want to do, we've done something that was not our responsibility to do, we've ignored our own needs and wants, and we get angry about it. To complicate matters, this victim, this poor person we've res-

cued, is not grateful for our help. He or she is not appreciative enough of the sacrifice we have made. The victim isn't behaving the way he or she should. This person is not even taking our advice, which we offered so readily. This person is not letting us fix that feeling. Something doesn't work right or feel right, so we rip off our halos and pull out our pitchforks. (22)

Without trying to speak for my brother, I can describe what I have personally observed in his life. I believe he was codependent on my dad, because along with me, he played the role of rescuer over and over—much more often than I did. I can attest to the fact that my brother got very angry with Dad on hundreds of occasions up until the last months of Dad's life. This anger was justified, but it was anger all the same, and it was damaging. My brother let my dad affect him dramatically, which in turn affected his health and the health of his marriage—which only stands to reason, since up until his death my dad lived in the same house with my brother and his wife.

I am happy to say that my brother got the help he needed, and much of the stress on his marriage was relieved after my dad's passing; but there is no question that my dad's disorder greatly influenced almost every decision made in Steve's household, as well as the atmosphere he and Angie lived in. Steve is still healing from the aftermath of sixty-plus years of life with Les.

As for me, well, I got a dose of reality when I read the following quote: "I'm not happy living with this person, but I don't think I can live without him." How many times had I said these very words to my closest friends, my children, and my spouse! As I stared at this sentence in *Codependent No More*, I realized just how very codependent I was. (23)

CONTROL

The list below is from the same book and is a partial picture of how I saw myself, either during my growing-up years, or as a married adult still dealing with and affected by my dad:

- A codependent is someone who has lived through events and with people who were out of control, causing the codependent sorrow and disappointment.

- A codependent is someone who has become afraid to let other people be who they are and allow events to happen naturally.

- A codependent is someone who doesn't see or deal with their fear of loss of control.

- A codependent is someone who thinks they know best how things should turn out and how people should behave.

- A codependent is someone who will try to control events and people through guilt, advice-giving, manipulation, and domination.(24)

Whereas my brother's codependency exhibited itself in rescuing and anger, my primary codependency trait was control. Yes, I rescued as well, but I did so because I needed to control the situation; I needed to make sure everything would turn out right. I took control by completing a project when Dad left things half done, such as the unfinished kitchen. When Dad checked out and our future was at stake, I took control, as I did when overseeing the move from Vance Street. I developed such a strong sense of control that it became second nature to me. I didn't even know I was doing it; I just thought I was surviving.

My need for control stemmed from the fact that I felt out of control growing up with a bipolar dad, and was exacerbated by some other painful and life-changing experiences over which I had little or no control. The sexual molestation by my Uncle Fred was one such experience. Not being able to control my dad's extravagant spending, which put us in the poor house of debt, was another experience. As a mom, I could not control outcomes to challenges my children were facing. I realized I needed to quit caring so much. I worked hard at this with my children and made great strides. I could only hope they would notice.

Learning to care less can be very liberating, but it takes a lot of work. I found myself caring almost too little. I became apathetic. Apathy is just another form of control. I struggled to find the balance between caring too much and not caring enough; I knew it would take a lifetime of work. Another area in need of some attention was my marriage. I had cared too much about the need for Clay and I to be united in thought about everything; it would take a good shaking up before I realized that we might never be on the same page, and that it was okay if we weren't. Until I learned that lesson, there were some very rocky stretches—so rocky, in fact, that I didn't think we would survive.

Clay and I had been married for a quarter of a century before we had our first big fight. He had let things get out of hand at the office. He had always been great with his hands, which made him a wonderful doctor of dental surgery, but running a business was not his strong suit. He was also not good at confrontation, and tended to ignore bad situations in the hope they would go away. He didn't understand that ignoring a problem only made the final outcome worse. Because he overlooked certain practices at the office, and failed to give proper guidance to his staff, we found ourselves in a big mess when his office "manager" (who didn't manage at all) decided to take another job. I had to fill in until we found a replacement, and what I discovered practically sent me to the loony bin.

The lady who had taken care of all his insurance claims and collections had neglected her job, leaving over thirty-thousand dollars in revenue uncollected. Not only that, but she had conspired with two other employees to take advantage of their laid-back boss by doing as little as possible. This did not sit well with my solid work ethic, but my bringing the problem to Clay's attention did not sit well with him. He did not want to be made aware of anything that would require a face to face. Instead of addressing the problems with staff and helping me sort out the mess, he hit the golf course.

I had just spent the previous year planning and overseeing the construction of a beautiful new dental building for Clay, and then decorating its interior myself. I knew that if we didn't get the financial part of the office in shape, we might well sink. But not only was I getting no cooperation from Clay, I was spending literally every waking hour at the office trying to collect the money owed us, and reorganizing the entire office protocol for greater efficiency. I had to research and contact over fifty insurance brokers to negotiate new contracts and chart their policies. I had to make an office manual from scratch and implement it. I had to learn to master a very difficult software program, and I had to hire and train three new employees in less than two months. I also had to make appointments, buy supplies, do monthly billing, send out reminder cards, prepare next-day clinical files, file patients' charts, and clean the office.

I started my day at six in the morning and got home at midnight. Sometimes I had so much to do that I worked through the night and slept on Clay's couch in his office. I was eating and sleeping poorly, gained ten years in age, and lost over twenty pounds; my clothes were falling off. I wasn't getting any exercise or seeing anyone outside of work. I felt like I was fighting single-handedly for the life of a business we had worked hard to build for twenty years, and Clay just let me do it, unaware that I was sinking rapidly.

I resented Clay for what was going on at the office, and I resented the fact that he had a better relationship with the kids, even though I loved and looked out for them just as much. We had several fights about these things, but the bigger fight was over our faith.

When Clay began questioning his choice of church, and moved in a very different direction from what we had married into I was beside myself. I tried to control that part of Clay; I begged, pleaded, cried, argued, screamed, and debated with Clay over every statement of belief. It was irritating how affable Clay was about it all. He never raised his voice or shouted back. He was happy. He had found what he had been looking for all his life, and he wasn't going to budge. I felt abandoned. He had left me for another, only it wasn't another woman, it was a thing. A thing I couldn't see or touch or even shoot.

He was so satisfied, in fact, that he never argued or tried to convince me; he never yelled or got frustrated. It didn't seem to matter to him that I was doing all of the above. He squelched every outrage with his silence. The silence killed my soul. I would have rather had the conversation, no matter how heated, than the perceived indifference. I knew in my heart of hearts what a good man Clay was, but I was too hurt to acknowledge it openly. I was both mad and confused about these changes, and I wanted no one else to know.

I suppose it was pride that made me want to keep Clay's new beliefs a secret. When Clay and I married, our faith guided every decision we made, including where we lived and what we did. It was our faith that led us to a small island in the Caribbean where Clay operated a benevolent clinic, supported by a well-known and respected religious organization, whose tenets we believed and taught. Not only was the religious organization we worked for well respected, but so were we. We were loved and admired for the benevolent work we did, and for the faith that propelled us to do it.

For Clay there was no trauma involved in changing his religion; he had been on a faith journey all his life, changing belief systems the way some people change jobs. I, on the other hand, had settled into my beliefs at twelve years of age, and hadn't wavered an inch since the day I made my first profession. My faith was everything to me, and I was convinced beyond a shadow of a doubt that what I believed was true.

Had it not been for my faith (and my church), I am confident I would not have survived growing up with a bipolar dad. When all hell was breaking loose at 1191 Vance Street, I made my way to a little piece of heaven on Bellevue Boulevard where I was loved, cared for, and taught about a Father who was perfectly good. It was my church that had helped me stay positive in a negative situation. It was my church that made me feel good about myself, no matter my background or the experiences I encountered. My youth group gave me purpose and hope for a better future, where I could leave behind all that was ugly, and move toward all that was good. Without this faith, I was nothing—or so I thought. It would take my own deconstruction to realize how much of my faith was real, and how much was simply what I had been taught. But I wouldn't understand about that until much later, after I had been through five very disappointing and lonely years.

Not only did I feel all alone, I felt worthless. I could not get past my past. I had been verbally abused by my dad, sexually abused by a relative, raised in a dysfunctional home that left me feeling vulnerable on every front, and had now reached middle age where I felt like a failure. I had lived the first half of my marriage, and all of my mothering, in a religious bubble that gave me boundaries, and provided an air of respectability, which I wore like a badge of honor. But it now seemed like a hollow achievement. I felt empty inside. What happened to the oneness I had once known with my husband? What happened to the happiness I had once enjoyed as a mother of four babies? What happened to the joy I had experienced as a person whose beliefs inspired service to others? Had everything been for nothing?

I felt broken, but I so desired to be fixed. I just didn't know how. It was during this time that Clay became my biggest cheerleader. His sympathetic ear and words of encouragement proved more valuable than all the sermons I had heard for the past forty years. Clay's very life was a sermon, demonstrated everyday with humility and grace. The girls at the office experienced his fairness, his patients appreciated his integrity, and a small community of battered women loved him for his.generosity and compassion.

For over ten years Clay had been involved in a ministry that helped women with addictions get back on their feet and start a new life. Abused women who had come from broken homes. Vulnerable women who had been taken advantage of by men. Women who had made bad choices in their loneliness and despair. When Clay started volunteering his time for the Women of Hope, little did he know that ten years down the road, his wife would become one of them. Clay's biggest challenge was no longer at the center, but at home with me. Clay's patient understanding began a rocky recovery with many ups and downs, but at least he gave me the courage to start the journey.

THE STORM

It wasn't long, however, before another storm blew into our lives which had a huge impact on the way I viewed life. Early one morning in the middle of trying to make sense of my life, I discovered a bump on the side of my head just above my ear; it turned out to be a soft-tissue sarcoma. I was told by my doctor that this type of cancer was extremely rare, and accounted for less than three percent of cancers, of which less than one percent are located in the head. When the doctor told me I had cancer, I didn't even cry; I was in shock. He told me on a routine visit when I was alone, and I made the two-hour trip back home in a daze. An angel must have guided me on the interstate, because I don't even remember holding the wheel.

I was too limp to pick up the phone and ring Clay. When I got back into town, I did call him and give him the news. He was also in shock, but found the strength to be tender and positive. I tried to talk about options, including funeral arrangements, which he firmly and quickly dismissed. It was a long month as we waited for all the tests to reveal the extent of the cancer. The good news was that a series of scans confirmed I did not have cancer anywhere else in my body; the bad news was that because I was going to have radiation treatments directly on my head, I would permanently lose a good portion of my hair.

Hearing that I would permanently lose my hair sent me further into depression. My family tried to cheer me up by telling me that hair was just hair, and the important thing was that with surgery and radiation, I could be cured, and live a long and happy life. Of course they were right, but at the time it was not what I wanted to hear. I wanted them to understand how devastating this was to me. The more they tried to make light of it, the more despondent I became.

My cancer journey actually turned out to be a healing of the soul, as well as the body. I was so consumed with surgery, radiation, and treatments that I had little time to think about much of anything except survival, and trying to get up enough energy to put one foot in front of the other. After spending five to six hours every day traveling back and forth to the cancer center, where I was bolted to a hard flat table, suffocated with a green plastic mask, and left alone to hear the surging sounds of the radiation penetrating my scalp, I was too exhausted to contend with anyone about anything. What little energy I did have left was spent in doctoring my overcooked head.

Six months after my surgery, I was still trying to regain my strength and physical appearance. I spent hours researching how to fix my hair, and after much trial and error I finally came up with a nice way to style it so that the large bald spot on one side did not show. As far as my inner self was concerned, I had become more open to new ideas, but I still struggled with understanding many of Clay's beliefs. The funny thing was, I no longer cared. I had no desire to contend or control; the need to control had been radiated out of me. In fact, almost every emotion I had, whether it was anger, fear, frustration, remorse, sadness, or regret, had slowly dissipated with each hair that had fallen from my head. I had become a zombie. I had no opinions or declarations, no driving purpose, no doctrine to die on a hill for.

When I lost my desire to try to change Clay's beliefs and actions, I also lost a piece of myself. Just as Clay had questioned everything he had learned both spiritually and morally, I began to do the same. Not that Clay had become amoral; he just had more compassion for the immoral. He never endorsed breaking the law; he just had more grace for the lawbreaker. He didn't see things as black and white; there was a lot more gray, and everyone, according to Clay, had a story, a reason for who they were, and what they did.

I didn't know how I was supposed to feel about much of anything. My awareness of my vulnerabilities reminded me that I needed to be less judgmental and more gracious. Clay had certainly demonstrated this kind of spirit. There had been a lot of things about Clay I did not understand, but these traits I not only admired, I envied. I desired to be like Clay in this way. To love myself without condemnation, to remove self righteous perceptions from my viewfinder, and to love others unconditionally. As I lay in bed recovering from my daily treatments, I picked up an imaginary mirror and took a good look at the mother, daughter, and wife staring back.

Looking into the mirror of my past made me realize that every aspect of my life had been subject to my tendency to take charge, and make sure things were done right in order to achieve good outcomes. I had tried to control too much with my children. Most of the time it was subtle and non-combative, but it was there at the core of my personality.

I thought about my dad, and how even as a young adult I had tried to control him. Everything was so out of control with him that I had to take charge in order to survive. It was a pattern I carried over into my relationship with my husband, and when I finally realized that truth, it made me sad. I did not want to be a controlling wife, to stress out when things didn't go the way I thought best. I really wanted to let go, but I was always afraid of the consequences. I was a very capable person, and it was extremely difficult to give up control when faced with the prospect of loss. As Beattie points out, "Perhaps the most painful loss many codependents face is the loss of our dreams, the hopeful and sometimes idealistic expectations for the future that most people have."(25)

I thought about that, and I realized she was right. Giving up control did mean the possibility of giving up my dreams. Dreams I had for the kids, dreams I had for my husband and me. Dreams of a good, safe, and normal life, unlike the one I had lived on Vance Street. Giving up control meant taking a chance on those dreams not coming to life. It meant accepting that things might not turn out the way I wanted or expected, that I might be disappointed. I thought about disappointment, and I remembered something Brene Brown had written in her book, *Rising Strong:*

> Disappointment is unmet expectations, and the more significant the expectations the more significant the disappointment… We have the tendency to visualize an entire scenario or conversation or outcome, and when

> things don't go the way we'd imagined, disappointment can become resentment. This often happens when our expectations are based on outcomes we can't control, like what other people think, what they feel, or how they're going to react.(26)

I had dreams. I had expectations. And I had disappointments that led to resentments. The resentments led to sadness, and the sadness led to a depressed state of mind. I never let on, as I put my acting skills to work whenever I stepped out of the house. It took a toll on me, however, and I knew I couldn't go on like that. Clay knew it as well.

It was a painful deconstruction but I finally realized I was the one who had to change, and gradually I reached the point where I was able to let go. Circumstances beyond my control had forced me to deal with my problem. I began the process of allowing other people to make their own choices and live with the outcomes, good or bad. I learned the hard lesson of allowing life to flow naturally without trying to control every step of the journey.

Reading the book *Loving What Is*, by Byron Katie, helped me put into practice the discipline of "letting go." It offered practical advice, positive steps, and clear explanations like the following:

> Much of our stress comes from mentally living out of our own business. When I think, "You need to get a job, I want you to be happy, you should be on time, you need to take better care of yourself," I am in your business. … If you are living your life, and I am mentally living your life, who is living mine? We're both over there. Being mentally in your business keeps me from being present in my own. I am separate from myself, wondering why my life doesn't work. To think that I know what's best for anyone else is to be out of my business. Even in the name of love, it is pure arrogance, and the result is tension, anxiety, and fear. Do I know what's right for me? That is my only business. Let me work with that before I try to solve your problems for you. (27)

Letting go and letting my husband and children control their own destinies was actually very liberating. It certainly freed me from the stress I put on myself to fix everyone's problems and arrange everyone's life. I learned to mind my own business, and let my family members mind theirs. It is true that I was still affected by their choices, for no one can expect to live an isolated life. Each of us is affected in some way by choices others make. Being able to face that reality with faith instead of fear is what brought me peace. When I refused to allow myself to get wrapped up in the lives of the people I was trying to control, it gave me the opportunity to live and enjoy my own.

Understanding my codependency, my control issues, and my rescuing tendencies was life-changing. It took a long time for me to recognize these traits. Codependency can be extremely damaging, but once I recognized the problem and took the needed steps to rescue myself from this crippling and dysfunctional pattern, life became better. Recognition was the first step; getting help was the second. But the third step was the hardest: I had to deal with my feelings, feelings I had repressed for years and couldn't quite pin down, feelings I had hidden behind walls to keep the real me inside where no one could see. I had to dig deep and break down the walls that had kept me safe.

THE FEELINGS

Over the years I had built walls to hide my true feelings of shame and hurt. I had buried them so deeply that it took years for them to surface. I learned to ignore my feelings by example, watching my mom, and I learned to keep quiet about them by instruction. "Children are to be seen and not heard," was my dad's policy, and I listened and obeyed.

And in a home where Hollywood was glorified and played out every day, I developed the acting skills necessary to cover up my feelings.

When there were fights between my brother and Dad, or between my grandmother, mother, and Dad, I sat in the corner and retreated into my own little world. Sometimes I retreated into my bedroom where I blocked out the situation. I covered my walls with pictures of movie stars, and pretended I was one of them, living a different life in a different world. Sometimes I escaped to the activities at our church. I went there as often as I could to skate and bowl; it was a positive place, where people really seemed to care about me. They didn't know my dad or my family situation, and I took care to keep it that way.

The activities I participated in at church were my refuge; I became my best self there. I never let on that our family had problems. In fact, everyone at church thought I had a Pollyanna existence. I became a very good actress, carrying this persona all the way through high school and college, and it served me well. At the time I didn't realize I was acting; I thought I had simply found a way to be normal.

I also never realized I was building walls. I don't even know when that began, although I can remember blocking out the pain, numbing my emotions so that I didn't feel anything. And I can remember feeling as if I were living two separate lives: one life at home, and another whenever I walked out the front door of my apartment at 1191 Vance Street. I had learned early in my growing-up years how to shut the door to one existence, and open the door to another.

Melody Beattie says that when we repress our feelings, "we may feel somewhat detached from ourselves, and our emotional responses may be flat, nonexistent, or inappropriate (laughing when we should be crying; crying when we should be happy)."(28) Codependents go through stages much like the ones identified by Elizabeth Kubler-Ross on death and dying: denial, anger, bargaining, depression, and acceptance.(29) Repressed thoughts and feelings fall into the category of denial, and like dying are a result of experiencing loss.

Every time I felt a significant loss, I would deny and push down my feelings. The fact that I did not have a normal dad, that I could not control my environment, that my mother or brother were hurt by my dad's behavior—these were all losses I experienced. I felt loss whenever my dad attacked me with words that made me feel hollow inside. I felt loss when I made mistakes that stripped me of my self-worth. Sometimes I got angry, and sometimes I became introspective and melancholy, but most of the time I repressed my feelings.

Repressed feelings never go away. They are buried deep within us, and stay there until we have the courage to dig them up and examine them honestly. Why is it so important to resurrect them? Because feelings are energy. Good feelings give us positive energy, and bad feelings give us negative energy. Even feelings we've long since forgotten about can sap our energy unless we bring them to the surface and deal with them. As Steven Tracy explains,

Facing our brokenness forces us to live in the truth, and helps us to identify and extinguish the destructive lies created by the shame of our abuse. Thus looking at our painful past is necessary for correcting the distorting effects of shame... Facing the truth and the pain of our past is also necessary in order to experience appropriate, healthy relationships.(30)

Repressed feelings are always negative. Why would we hide a positive feeling? Therefore, any feeling that is repressed is going to have a negative impact on us. It will affect our decisions, the way we view relationships, the way we understand our life and our world. Given this fact, it is crucial to deal with repressed feelings. But dealing with them is not pleasant. It is extremely difficult and taxing, because it takes us to a place of vulnerability.

Vulnerability is a sister to depression, the fourth stage identified by Elizabeth Kubler-Ross. On occasion I did experience the second stage, anger, and I'm sure I bargained (the third stage) at some point in my life, although I can't recall it. But I remember the vulnerability quite well. Not only did I feel vulnerable as a young girl growing up on Vance Street; I felt vulnerable trying to resurrect the hidden feelings I had kept buried. I had buried them for a reason, and the thought of digging them up was not a happy one. "When we were children, we used to think that when we were grown up we would no longer be vulnerable. But to grow up is to accept vulnerability. To be alive is to be vulnerable."(31)

Brene Brown describes vulnerability as "uncertainty, risk, and emotional exposure," and associates it with love in the following way: "Waking up every day and loving someone who may or may not love us back, whose safety we can't ensure, who may stay in our lives or may leave without a moment's notice, who may be loyal till the day they die or betray us tomorrow—that's vulnerability."(32)

My earliest memory of my dad leaving causes some of my deeply buried feelings of love and fear to surface. I loved my dad enough to run after him; I feared he didn't love us enough to return. Loving someone so much, only to fear they may not love you back, was a feeling I didn't want to have, so I buried it. Knowing that if my dad walked out on us once he might do it again (which he did, several times) gave rise to another feeling: a feeling of abandonment.

Other feelings I had buried were those related to my personal inadequacies. I buried them as quickly as possible, covering them with laughter and humor, but they were there just the same. I thought about that quite a bit, and realized that I was a birthed reflection of my dad's insecurities. He felt as if he never measured up, and had unwittingly projected those feelings onto those of us who lived with him. When it came to my dad's enterprises, it was typical for them to start out as something good and hopeful, but end in regret. This pattern repeated itself over and over and led to another feeling within me: a feeling of insecurity. Whenever Dad started a new venture I would get nervous. Because Dad's adventures usually put us deeper in debt, I was always anxious about his excitement over a new business opportunity, and wondered if we would have enough money to live on. And whenever Dad's businesses failed, I had yet another feeling: shame.

I had to take a good look at these resurrected feelings—feelings of fear, inadequacy, insecurity, shame, abandonment, and being unloved—and deal with them. These were the feelings that haunted me all my life, and I had to examine each one, and face the reality of how it had affected me. This process made me feel vulnerable for several reasons: it meant admitting that I had issues with self-esteem. It meant admitting some things that might cost me the respect of people who had seen me as a strong and faithful person. But I chose vulnerability, and exposed past feelings that were affecting the present. I knew that those feelings needed to be brought into the light of day before they could be buried for good in another plot. So, one by one, I looked deeply into these past feelings, their meaning for me, and how they were related to my experience. I made a list:

- *Fear.* Fear is actually the mother of all the other feelings. It is what gives birth to inadequacy, insecurity, shame, abandonment, and the feeling that I am unloved. Get rid of fear and the feelings below crumble.

- *Inadequacy.* Am I pretty enough? Am I smart enough? Am I athletic enough? Will my children be healthy? Will my children be smart? Will they be "enough"?

- *Insecurity.* My insecurities were mainly economic and social. Will I have a place to live? Will I get the job? Will my husband make enough money? Will my children be able to support themselves? Will my children find purpose?

- *Shame.* Will my dad embarrass me? Will my dad fail again? Will I fail again? Will I embarrass my husband? Will I embarrass my children?

- *Abandonment.* Will my dad leave us? Will I please my husband? Will my children move away? Will my children stay in touch?

- *Unloved.* Will I get married? Will my children love me? Will my children find love? Will my children be happy?

As I listed these feelings, I saw the pattern: every feeling I had repressed as a child, I had regurgitated as an adult, not only for myself, but for my children. After I identified these feelings, it became clear to me why I acted so crazy sometimes. I had carried my childhood fears over into my marriage, and into my motherhood.

The first step in overcoming the negative feelings was to face the reality that they were present. That made it easier to identify them when they showed themselves in day-to-day living. The next step was to practice thinking the opposite of the feeling. Believing the good about something as opposed to believing the worst.

The third step was to turn the negative into a positive with my words. This was a very hard thing to do, and took great discipline and constant effort. I really tried not to put myself down, even in fun. I paid a great deal of attention to my storytelling, trying to catch myself when I was being negative about one of the children or Clay. I worked on not being cynical or sarcastic. I worked on not saying anything that sounded like a judgment. I was careful not to use words that carried the emotions of doubt or fear. Charles Capps puts it this way: "Words are containers. They carry faith, or fear, and they produce after their kind."(33) I soon learned that the best way to watch my words was to use very few: quiet, I discovered, isn't so bad after all.

The last step was to remember that most of the negatives we believe about ourselves are lies. Life has so many more positives to offer than negatives! I began asking the question, "Do I know for certain that what I fear is true or will come to pass?" If I couldn't say yes, then I worked at removing the fear, and replacing it with the expectation or hope of a positive outcome. I would also remember where I'd come from, and think about how far I'd come. When a feeling of fear crept into my heart concerning one of my children, I would remind myself that I had made it just fine, and so could they.

I allowed myself to face my fears, face my feelings, and become vulnerable to my family and friends. I quit trying to be perfect. I quit trying to hide the fact that my children were not perfect. It was amazing how much energy I reclaimed. It had taken so much energy to try to have the perfect family, the perfect Christmas, the perfect vacation, and the perfect home! It had worn me out, and I was too tired to fake it any longer. I finally quit acting…and started accepting.

ACCEPTANCE

The last stage of grief identified by Elizabeth Kubler-Ross is acceptance. This is the last stage a codependent will embrace before his/her soul is mended. We must all reach a state of acceptance in order for life to have meaning, or at the very least, sanity. Melody Beattie explains it best in *Codependent No More*:

> We are at peace with what is. We are free to stay, free to go on, free to make whatever decisions we need to make. We are free! We have accepted our loss, however minor or significant. It has become an acceptable part of our present circumstances. We are comfortable with it and our lives. We have adjusted and reorganized. Once more, we are comfortable with our present circumstances and ourselves.
>
> Not only are we comfortable with our circumstances and the changes we have endured, but we believe we have in some way benefitted from our loss or change, even if we cannot fully understand how or why. We have faith that all is well, and we have grown from our experience. We deeply believe our present circumstances—every detail of them

—are exactly as they ought to be for the moment. In spite of our fears, feelings, struggles, and confusion, we understand everything is okay even if we lack insight. We accept what is. We settle down. We stop running, ducking, controlling, and hiding. And we know it is only from this point that we can go forward.(34)

Acceptance means coming to terms with behaviors and circumstances *that we cannot change*. As a child I had to put up with unacceptable behavior because I had no choice; that was the family into which I had been born. I could have been born into a nicer situation, or a much worse situation, but I learned to accept just what I had been given. Growing up a religious person, I believed (and still do) that my Creator was overseeing my situation and taking care of me. For every sadness I experienced, there was a hope within me that one day all would be well. Most importantly, I believed that by the grace of God, the mayhem was serving a purpose; I believed God was doing something in me, and that somehow, some way, I would be a better person for it. That being said, it still was never easy.

Acceptance does not mean that we put up with unacceptable behavior if we have a choice. There were times I wanted so much for my mom to stand up to my dad, and not allow him to talk to her the way he did, but that was not for me to decide. When I was older, however, I chose on many occasions to remove myself from my dad's presence so he could not berate me.

Acceptance does not mean we do nothing. Steve and I grew up with very little, so we worked hard as adults to make something of ourselves. We both worked our way through college, bought our own cars, paid for our own weddings, bought our own houses, paid our own bills, and paid for our children's education—and then we took care of our parents. Neither Steve nor I ever started a project we didn't finish. As dependents we had been obliged to accept quite a bit, but as independents we were not; we took charge of our lives and made them work for us.

Acceptance does mean we grieve loss. I came to the reality that I had loss in my life, and instead of denying it, I embraced it, and made time to mourn. Psychologists tell us that it is healthy to grieve. They tell us that grief is an important and genuine emotion which, if denied, can take a toll on us physically.(35) As a child I did not understand the importance of mourning a loss, but I mourned naturally, retreating to my room many evenings to cry for no apparent reason. Now I know the reason. Similarly, during my five-year depression I cried almost every day, but because I was unable to identify the repressed feelings, I never knew why I was crying; I just knew I was sad. Healthy acceptance came when I understood the reason for my grief.

Contemplative prayer was an important part of my acceptance as well. Richard Rohr, in his book *Everything Belongs*, describes this kind of soul-searching awareness:

> As we move into a contemplative stance, it becomes clear that we determine by our internal dialogue and predispositions—fears, angers, and judgments—much more than we'd like to admit. We determine what we will see and what we won't see, what we pay attention to and what we don't. That's why we have to clean the lens: we have to get our ego-agenda out of the way, so we can see things as they are. ... If our reality is negative, we will avoid that part of it. We need a broader lens, which is actually just a cleaner one. The truth is always too much for our ego. Who is ready for the whole truth? I'm not. For the thinking of the ego is largely based on fear. Fear of what I might not be. Fear of what I might see. Fear I won't be successful or accepted, or that I will be hurt. So we have to recognize how dominant fear is in our lives. ... But love is who we really are. We'll never see the love we really are, our foundation, if we keep living out of our false self of self-protection and overreaction. We must remember that "perfect love casts out fear."(36) (37)

Acceptance is learning to see things as they really are, through a clean lens that has had fear, judgment, anger, bitterness, and loathing wiped from its surface and sees through the eyes of love. The verse Rohr quotes from the Bible is a simple one, but it packs a wallop: perfect love really does cast out fear. When we know we are loved, we can face just about anything. Growing up, I knew God loved me, and I knew He loved me perfectly. That is what got me through the hard times.

As I matured, I came to understand that people are not like God: they will not love perfectly, and will often let you down. On the other hand, their love will often rise higher than you thought possible. The important thing is to clean the lens through which you view them, and in this way, gain a truer perspective. Through a clearer lens I saw how much my dad loved me, and my fears of abandonment gradually subsided.

The other feelings, feelings of insecurity, inadequacy, and shame, were not so easily rooted out. It has taken much time to understand them, and even more time to accept the loss they represented. I have come a long way, and am a much different person than I was six years ago, but the feelings still surface from time to time. I continue to practice what I have learned during my "healing." It is not a given that once you are healed it is over. You are constantly in healing mode, with an ongoing awareness of the need to forgive others, forgive yourself, accept reality, reject lies, and let go of what you have no control over. It is the only way out of the bondage of depression and fear.

It is equally important to understand that whether we have been victimized or not, we do not have to remain victims. It is important to realize, too, that some of our pain was brought about by our own choices. When we admit our part in our pain, we free ourselves from the belief that we are victims of fate—a belief that keeps us in bondage. Taking responsibility is an honest admission that we chose certain paths that led to certain outcomes. Not everything that happened to us was someone else's fault; not every painful experience was forced upon us by circumstances, outsiders, or the Almighty. Some of our own decisions played a significant role in our destiny. It is important to understand all this, as long as we don't live in regret.

Once we own that concept, we are well on our way to freedom. Understanding the truth of the human condition will allow us to let go of the idea that we should expect perfection from ourselves and others. When we take responsibility for at least some aspects of our pain, and then release ourselves from the guilt of bad choices, we can have peace to move forward, right wrongs by learning from our past, and make a better future for ourselves and those we love.

Is this easy? Absolutely not! It is an ongoing up-and-down journey of faith and discipline. It is tiring to the point of exhaustion. Progress comes with blood, sweat, and tears. At times the difficulty of the journey can bring you down, but if you really want to be free, you will rise and try again. It is a battle, and as with every battle, you must ask yourself whether the outcome is worth the effort. My patriotic veteran dad used to say to me, "Freedom isn't free." He was right. It takes hard work to become free and stay free. But the freedom is worth every bit of it!

LIFE BECAUSE OF LES

THE GRANDKIDS

There was much about my dad that was good. In writing about my healing I have painted a somewhat dark picture of him. I am sure that my friends, who only saw his happy side, would be shocked to read what I have written (which is part of my being vulnerable). If, when reading this, you find yourself feeling confused by the ambiguity of my life with Les, then you have a taste of what it was like to live with him.

The stories I shared are all true and represent the best and worst of my dad. I have not exaggerated his anger, verbal abuse, failures, or sadness; nor have I exaggerated my pain. Having said that, it would not be fitting if I failed to end this story with an account of the wonderful ways in which my dad impacted our lives. With all the hurt and pain my brother and I encountered, we experienced an equal amount of happiness and love, as well as an approach to life that not many have the opportunity to appreciate.

This approach to life was passed down to our children. Each of my children and my brother's only child inherited wonderful talents from my dad, whether through birth or as learned behaviors; either way, they were definitely a result of life with Les. I have already mentioned my nephew's artistic ability. He was probably closer to my dad than all the other children, having grown up with his Papa in the same household. Although an only child, Jack was not brought up as one; he had to share life with two older "siblings," siblings that were 70 years his senior. Jack learned much from his live-in grandparents.

Dad spent hundreds of hours playing board games with Jack, and Jack became a game master. When he went off to college there was no one who could beat him at any table or card game. He learned to think quickly, analytically, and decisively as a result of all the time my dad spent with him, playing simple but competitive games; it was during these one on ones that Dad passed down wisdom and knowledge as only a grandfather can do.

Although my children did not get to spend as much time with Dad as Jack did, they still benefitted from his many visits. Dad wanted to be with all the grandkids as much as possible. While he was employed by Pony Express he made it a point to drop by our home every time his work brought him anywhere close enough to rationalize a visit. Michael was only two then, but Dad would take time out from his schedule of deliveries to stop by and take him for a stroll. As the eldest, Michael probably has the most vivid memories of both the good and the bad; I can only hope he remembers more of the positives than the negatives.

Whether he would admit it or not, he learned a great deal from my dad.

Like his grandfather, Michael became a hopeless romantic, an aspect of my dad that was revealed to me through stories my mom still loves to recall. Just the other day while staying with me for a few weeks, she told me again about the beautiful love letters he wrote to her during the war. Never one to do anything in an ordinary way, Les Ash always sketched cartoon pictures on the outside of the envelope: lovesick soldiers pining for their gal; cupids and fairies; himself on one side of the envelope, and my mom on the other. The artwork was always colorful and detailed, and every letter (there were at least a dozen) was different and adorably creative. My mom cherished each one, stashing them in a cigar box for safekeeping. Even the mailman went out of his way to personally hand-deliver these beautifully crafted letters to her.

My dad's romantic nature was something that never left him. My brother and I saw this in him during our growing-up years, and as a result we both became hopeless romantics ourselves. Dad was in love with beauty, music, science, art, nature, and certain people. Seeing things through the eyes of a romantic brings with it emotional highs and lows. We got our passion from our dad, who could sink as low as he could soar high.

It is this passion and romance that was passed down to Michael. I never fully realized this until I saw how he pursued the love of his life. Like his grandfather, he too was proficient in making his love known to his beautiful wife. It was his sensitivity to beauty and his creative expressions of love that won her heart; he used art, music, and poetry to make her fall in love with him, and like his grandfather, he was tender and sweet. Unlike his grandfather, however, he never felt he had anything to prove, and that proved to be his most endearing quality of all.

My youngest son, Elliot, has winning ways, is ingenious, and is not afraid to take risks. No question where he got that: no one was more daring than my dad. I think Dad sometimes did dangerous things to overcome his fears. While a pilot serving in the Air Corps he would often take his plane out on unauthorized and dangerous maneuvers. One of his favorite tricks was to fly as close to the hoods of cars as possible, so low that the drivers would cover their heads until he passed, and then do something much more expressive with their hands.

He also loved to fly under bridges and telephone wires just for the sheer excitement of it. One day while flying, he spotted a small patch of field surrounded by woods on all sides, and couldn't pass it up: he had to know if he could land in the field without crashing into the trees. He circled several times, calculating just how much space was needed for the landing, and then circled a few more times to work up his nerve. Finally he flew down with bated breath and landed his plane in the patch of field, bringing it to a screeching halt right in front of a tree.

He was very pleased with himself, until it hit him that he was going to have to take off again on a makeshift runway too short for what was needed. Not one to panic, he simply carried out his mathematical calculations once more, turned his plane in the opposite direction, and sped full throttle toward the trees ahead, accelerating the engine speed until the plane was shaking. At just the right moment he lifted off, tucking the wheels back into the undercarriage. He cleared the main branches of the trees, but managed to snag some of the smaller ones as he soared to safety.

This foolish act gave him a high he talked about for years. When he got back to the barracks he recounted the story over and over again to his delighted Air Corps buddies. These were the same ones who dared him into other shenanigans, some of which got him into trouble. Either my dad could not pass up a dare because he was so eager to be one of the guys, or he was trying to prove something to himself; probably a little of both. All the men liked him, so he didn't really need to do stupid things to win their friendship. That may have played a role, but I think the bigger incentive was to overcome some underlying inadequacy.

Elliot was very daring during his high school and college days. One Saturday while at the University of Tennessee he took several friends to a rock quarry located not far from campus. Two of the boys were upperclassmen like himself; the third was a freshman and the son of friends of ours. The quarry had a cliff that extended over a body of water eighty feet below. It also had a gate and a "Keep Out" sign posted in plain view, but the boys leapt over the gate and jumped off the cliff into the water. The upperclassmen tackled the challenge with ease, but the freshman was not so lucky. We got a call from Elliot that afternoon that sent chills up my spine: our friend's son had landed badly in the water, and they had called for an ambulance to come and take him to the hospital. He had broken his back.

Clay and I panicked as all kinds of scenarios played out in our minds. Would he live? Would he be paralyzed? How would his poor parents handle this? Was Elliot to blame? Thank goodness, the fall did not sever the boy's spinal cord, although he did have to drop out of school for a year, while he wore a brace to strengthen his spine and give the cord time to heal.

Needless to say, we determined to have a serious talk with our son about his part in this fiasco, but it was unnecessary; Elliot already felt horrible and took full responsibility for what had happened. He stayed with the freshman at the hospital until his parents could drive up, and then stayed with him as much as possible after they arrived.

Thankfully for all our sakes, the boy's parents never held the accident against Elliot or us. They were great about it; we were not so great about it.

Elliot was always living on the edge, which kept me on the edge, until he finally moved away from home to live with his brother in another state. It was there that he met his future wife, who settled him down. He began to exercise the more desirable aspect of this risk-taking character trait when he dared to take a chance in opening a small business. Like his grandfather before him, he had great ideas and the ambitious spirit of the entrepreneur. Unlike his grandfather, he coupled these traits with a fantastic work ethic, and made a great success of his business, which led to even greater career opportunities. He is well on his way to a very successful life.

My daughter, Noel, was quietly observant; I think she heard and saw more than I knew at the time. My dad was around for a good bit of Noel's young life, and she most likely overheard every conversation he and I had, or at least the retelling of them to my husband. She would have also heard some pretty lively discussions about all kinds of important topics and world events: my dad was very knowledgeable and gifted at expressing himself. Couple that with a huge dose of passion, and you have the makings of a lawyer, which is exactly what Noel aspired to become.

Les took the time to analyze details and study problems with great objectivity, coming up with well-thought-out and reasonable solutions. This was one of the sides of my dad I loved most. He was like this for only about one week out of every month, but during those golden times he allowed me to express my ideas and opinions; and he listened to them with understanding and respect. In these talks he taught me the art of reason, which I believe was passed down to Noel. Her critical thinking she got from her own father, but her reasoning skills, dialogue, and writing ability she got from our side of the family. She has used these gifts to great advantage in her law career.

Dad's creativity, romantic flair, adventurous spirit, zest for life, ability to reason, artistic talent, and even his devil-may-care attitude were just some of the traits he passed down to all of us. These were the positives. Our work ethic and drive were a result of the negatives: we had to do so much to rescue and take care of our dad, that in the process we became hardworking, driven individuals determined to make a good life for ourselves.

My brother and I went through some painful experiences, and yet we came out on the other side having gained something from them. The gift shop was one of those experiences. We learned how to buy and sell, how to move merchandise, how to deal with the public. We learned the importance of responsibility, and of finishing a project—any project, every project—and the value of family working together on those projects. We passed these ideals down to our own children.

MEMORY LANE

Our children can remember only what their grandfather was like as an old man. I remember a younger man who made life interesting and fun. When I think back to my very earliest years, I reflect on the little things we did together that made life good—things that make me smile when I close my eyes at night and remember our home on Vance Street. I remember how he made me feel safe. I recall him showing me how to catch a softball, float on my back, skate, and play kick the can. I remember the time he showed me how to make my voice vibrate as I sang into the large box fan in the hall window, and the times when it snowed, and he pulled me behind the car on a garbage can lid.

What else fills my memory? The mornings we went bowling in Crosstown, then crossed the street for a Dyer's hamburger, (Memphis style); the hot summer afternoons when he snuck us into hotel swimming pools; the evenings we danced together as he taught me how to jitterbug and foxtrot; the nights he played Monopoly with us until dawn. I remember him insisting on taking the side of the sidewalk closest to the curb when we walked down the street together, because that is what gentlemen do.

He was very keen on manners. Whenever a female of any age walked into the room, he stood; when he passed a lady on the street, he tipped his hat, and he gave up his seat on the bus to any woman or older man who was without one. He never missed a "God bless you" when someone sneezed, and made sure Steve and I always said, "Yes, ma'am" and "No, sir." He taught us to thank our mother and grandmother for dinner each night, to eat with our mouths closed, and to ask to be excused before leaving the table. Bodily noises were unacceptable, and we never discussed childbirth or sex. In the presence of adults we had to be respectful, polite, and quiet unless called upon to perform—although we were able to let our hair down, and act as crazy as we wanted when it was just our family. I am proud of Dad for his good "southern manners," as he called them. I think they went a long way in building our character.

In the early years, he was painstakingly meticulous, including the way he dressed. He had matching cuff links and tie clips, silk socks, and patent leather shoes. He had pinstriped suits with fat ties. And he had hairpieces that made him look ten years younger; I forget when he quit wearing those, but I think it was when he became the janitor of our apartment buildings.

When he taught me how to draw a face, he focused on the minute details of the character, and when he taught me how to sketch a horizon, the fine points of the drawing were what mattered. Every discussion on politics, philosophy, science, or history was backed by a multitude of relevant, precise, and interesting facts. Whenever I enlisted his help on a school project, it was this attention to particulars that helped me get an A. It's also what made him the best fake Santa in town, a role he continued to play every Christmas long after we stopped believing. It was Dad's passion for detail that made every holiday special.

Halloween, especially, brought out the kid in him. Mom called the other day to remind me of one occasion I had long since forgotten. I had invited several friends over for a party, and Dad decided he would make it the best Halloween ever. He spent all week creating a monkey's paw just for the event, a horrible thing made out of clay and what looked like rat's hair, with a blood-like substance painted on the wrist for effect. He got the reaction he was looking for: when he opened the box to show us the paw, everyone screamed and ran out of the house. I had to beg them to come back! Dad kept the paw for years; it somehow eluded all of Grandma's attempts to get rid of it, and kept resurfacing. I think she finally burned it.

Easter was also a big day for my dad. He had deeply spiritual experiences during Easter. I remember going with him one year to an outdoor Passion play and both of us crying. Every Easter Mom and Grandma made sure I had white shoes, white gloves, and a white purse, as well as a pink cotton dress with a white slip; Dad made sure we had an Easter egg hunt. Every year he put a five-dollar bill into a golden egg and hid it in a very hard-to-find location, which my brother invariably found. Dad organized Easter egg hunts right up until I was a senior in college; by that time my brother was long gone, and I was the one who got to spend the five.

Camping is another fond memory. Dad taught us how to put a worm on a hook and cast our lines into the water. Not that I ever caught a fish! After the thrill of fishing wore off, he had us look for all sizes of twigs, sticks, branches, and logs to build a fire; its construction was a work of art which had to be architecturally perfect. Once the fire was well established, we roasted hot dogs and marshmallows, and then set up our pup tents, and spent a sleepless night in the woods. Before going to bed, however, Dad would point out every constellation in the heavens, telling us its name and the astronomer who discovered it.

Dad loved to sing, especially in the car. On Sunday drives he would sing hymns he had learned as a child: "The Old Rugged Cross" and "I Come to the Garden Alone" were among his favorites. Before I had my own car he ferried me back and forth to college, and we would sing together to pass the time on the long drive. He loved to sing songs from the war years, and taught me several of the classics, such as "Chattanooga Choo Choo" and "Marie." It became almost a ritual for us, and once I had my own car I missed our melodious trips together.

Dad was pretty good at impersonations, and could do Edward G. Robinson, Jimmy Durante, James Cagney, and Dean Martin. He would recite poetry in Truman Capote style, or put a comb over his lip to do a Hitler impression. I remember eating TV dinners in the living room while watching Bonanza on Sunday nights. I remember crawling up on the couch beside him and brushing his hair. I remember holding a flashlight for him under the hood of a car in the middle of the night, and handing him tools as he worked on projects in the garage behind the house. I remember helping him fold and throw papers for Steve's paper route.

I remember putting on shows for him on the little stage he built in the garage. I remember eating watermelon with him at a picnic table on a summer day, and getting quarters from him for the ice cream truck that came by like clockwork on Saturdays. I remember he always wanted to hold me and never let me go. I remember his love.

Proverbs 10:12 says, "Love covers a multitude of wrongs." It is true that my brother and I have vivid memories of pain from our growing-up years, but we do not remember those moments with bitterness. Most of the time we speak of them with a mixture of laughter and pity. We have either blocked out or forgotten a good deal more than we have remembered. My dad cycled at least once a month, which puts the number of explosive episodes well into the hundreds; yet we remember only a handful.

My mom, the most victimized of the three of us, can't even remember the negative things Steve and I recall. She rarely talks about Dad's shortcomings unless I press her for stories. She remembers mostly his compassionate side and defends him relentlessly. Her love for Dad is clearly a tribute to the kind of person she is; but it is also a tribute to the kind of man Dad was, buried deep beneath his lifetime of pain.

In spite of the many negatives, Dad could be an upbeat and positive person. And in spite of the sadness associated with him, I have many happy memories. I know that my brother and Mom would concur. Life with Les was an extraordinary life that hugely impacted the way we think about living, the way we see our world, the way we see our neighbors, including those less fortunate than ourselves. It was a life that deepened our convictions about the importance of family, and has kept us from taking for granted the things we see, hear, taste, and feel, or the blessings we have been given. It was a life that brought us beauty, even out of pain.

If only our Dad had been able to realize what he had passed down to us, he would not have felt like such a failure. Perhaps he now knows. Perhaps he finally realizes he was a success after all.

EPILOGUE

It's been almost six years since I began the story about my dad. The writing was a way for me to deal with the sadness I felt after his death. As it turned out, the process became a kind of surgery for my soul, drawing out my own story of pain, survival, failure, and redemption. It is the story of a young girl who felt, "less-than," and a dad who felt, "never-was."

Near the end of my five-year depression I found myself spiraling down a dark hole to a bottomless pit of grief. I began to believe that the bipolar disorder that had crippled my dad had been passed down to me, and I struggled to gain perspective on my life. I questioned everything I had ever believed. Some of those beliefs were challenged and changed. Others were not. The most important belief that I was loved and accepted by my Creator was never lost. Much of my life's journey was filled with laughter and well-lit paths. Some of my journey was dark. The good that came out of the bad, however, was worth the heartache, and therefore I have no regrets for the experiences encountered along the way. I do not hold anyone accountable for their participation in that pain, nor do I judge them. The best part is I no longer judge myself.

I still struggle with many of the same issues that took me down to the pit of despondency, but the good news is that my recovery is much quicker now. I still struggle in my relationships with my children, but the good news is that I recognize more easily my own faults; and can chose to do the work to make things better. I still struggle with all the changes in Clay and my marriage, but the good news is that I can see the bigger picture more clearly and have hope.

Just the other day Clay gave me a song to listen to, telling me he thought it was written especially for me. I played it over and over as wet drops of self-acceptance trickled down my cheeks. He was right; it **was** a song written for me. Everything my husband had been trying to tell me for several years became crystal clear in the three minutes I sat listening. Here are the lyrics to that song:

> I am not disappointed in you;
> I never have been, and I never will be.
> I'm not embarrassed or confused,
> Thinking you better improve yourself
> Or else…I'm done with you.
>
> No, I'm not disappointed in you,
> I'm not ashamed of you, thinking what a letdown.
> I'm not frustrated or accusing, bitter or abusive.
> I am love, and I love you.

I'm not bored with you,
I'm celebrating you.
I have set you on a Rock,
A chip off the old block,
At home in this beautiful place.

Never doubting you,
No need to shout at you;
Hey, I think you're amazing,
Though sometimes a little crazy.
How I love to laugh with you.

I am not disillusioned with you;
I never had any illusions in the first place.
I know exactly who you are,
I've known you from the start.
Yes, I am love, and I love you.

(Godfrey Birtill, Whitefield Music UK © 2016
Admin songsolutions.org)

NOTES:

1) See Steven Tracy, "Mending the Soul" (Zondervan, 2005), pages 184-189
2) See "MTS" (Mending the Soul) page 184
3) See "MTS" page 185
4) See "MTS" page 186
5) See "MTS" page 190
6) This is an old saying I heard all my life and has no origin.
7) See "MTS" pages 135-136
8) See authors Mark Bauer, MD, Amy Kilbourne, PH.D., MPH, Devra Greenwald, MPH, Evette Ludman, PH.D., "Overcoming Bipolar Disorder" (New Harbinger, 2008), P 18
9) See "What are Neurotransmitters", www.Neurogistics.com/The Science/What areNeurotransmi09CE.asp
10) See "OBD" (Overcoming Bipolar Disorder) page 13
11) See "OBD" page 112
12) See "OBD" page 113
13) See "OBD" page 113
14) See Melody Beattie, "Codependent No More" (Hazelden Publishing,1992), 32-52
15) See "CNM" (Codependent No More) page 34
16) See "MTS" page 34
17) See "CNM" pages 41-50
18) See "CNM" page 34
19) See Webster's New World Pocket Dictionary, Fourth Edition (Wiley Publishing 2000)
20) See Webster's New World Pocket Thesaurus, Second Edition (Wiley Publishing 2000)
21) See "CNM" page 84
22) See "CNM" page 85
23) See "CNM" page 97
24) See "CNM" page 44
25) See "CNM" page 130
26) See Brene Brown, "Rising Strong" (Spiegel and Grau of Random House, 2015), p 139
27) See Byron Katie, "Loving What Is" (Three Rivers Press, 2002) page 3

28) See "CNM" page 135
29) See "CNM" page 134 on Elizabeth Kubler-Ross, "On Death and Dying" (New York: MacMillan Publishing, 1969)
30) See "MTS" pages 135-136
31) See Brene Brown, "Daring Greatly" (Avery Publishing, 2012), page 43
32) See "DG" page 34
33) See Charles Capps, "God's Creative Power" (Capps Publishing, 2004), p 8
34) See "CNM" page 137
35) See "CNM" page 139
36) See I John 4:18 from the Bible
37) See Richard Rohr, "Everything Belongs" (Crossroad Publishing, 2003),
98-99

Made in the USA
Middletown, DE
10 April 2021